A Token's View from inside the Internal Revenue Service

A Token's View from inside the Internal Revenue Service

Oscar Williams

toExcel

San Jose · New York · Lincoln · Shanghai

A Token's View from inside the Internal Revenue Service
Copyright © 2000 by Oscar Williams

ISBN: 0-595-00037-1

Published by Writers Club Press, an imprint of iUniverse.com, Inc.

For information address:
iUniverse.com, Inc.
620 North 48th Street
Suite 201
Lincoln, NE 68504-3467
www.iuniverse.com

URL: http://www.writersclub.com

Contents

Introduction

If you are looking for a book on taxes, you have selected the wrong book. This book is not about the IRS and taxes. This book is about attitude. IRS attitude. An organization is just like a person. It has an organizational personality. It has goals, likes and dislikes. When a person thinks of Disney, he conjures up a picture of Snow White and a feeling of trust and a rightness about things. When someone hears the words, Internal Revenue Service, often a cold sweat breaks out, he might glance over his shoulder and quicken his pace. If he conjures up an image, it will probably be that of a junk yard dog.

I worked for the IRS for the last seventeen years of my thirty-eight-year Federal service career. I was the Fiscal Officer (Comptroller) for the IRS's Fresno Service Center in Fresno, California. I got to study the beast from the inside. The title of my book, "A token's View From Inside the IRS,"came about when early in my tenure with the IRS I realized that I had been hired to add some color to the organization. I was their token black.

I developed a perception of the organization. The IRS is not paranoid because it believes everyone hates it. The truth is everyone in their right mind does hate it. It is constantly on the defense for demonstrating its black boots intimidation of citizens; illegally providing tax data

1

to the Executive Office; lying to the Congress; and entering into ill thought out programs, which waste billions of tax dollars.

What happens to a personality under constant stress? It often becomes schizophrenic (a psychotic disorder characterized by loss of contact with reality). In this book you will get to walk with me into the mind of a schizophrenic organization. A lot of what you read will sound like fictional comedy. There is no fiction in this book. Everything, as strange as it may seem is completely true. This following organization chart and a brief description of the functions of each segment of the IRS are provided in order to help the reader understand the organizational structure of the IRS and better visualize the hierarchy.

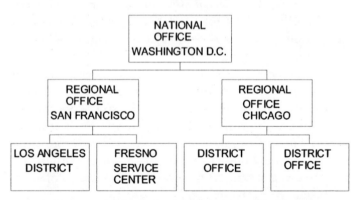

The National Office. The IRS is part of the Treasury Department. The Commissioner, a political appointee is the head of the organization. He is located in the National Office in Washington, D.C. He has a deputy who is a civil servant and in theory provides continuity to the organization as appointees come and go. Also, in the National Office are a bunch of assistants to the commissioner and associate commissioners. Basically these folks are just branch chiefs, i.e., the Equal Employment Opportunity Officer, the Public Affairs Officer, Computer Services etc. The function of the National Office is to coordinate with the Treasury Department, set policy for the IRS, and oversee the regional offices.

Regional Offices. There are nine regional offices under the National Office. These are spread throughout the United States and are responsible for a given geographic area. For example the Western Regional Office is located in San Francisco. It covers Idaho, Washington, Oregon, Alaska, Hawaii, Nevada and California. The head of each region is called a regional commissioner. Under the regional commissioner are assistant regional commissioners (ARC's) who head each office in the regional headquarters. For example there is the ARC for Collection and Taxpayer Service and one for Human Resources. Each office has a branch structure comparable to the National Office. In fact the heads of the branches in the regional offices are titled, branch chiefs. The functions of the regional offices are to coordinate between the National office and the districts which they oversee.

District Offices. There are sixty two-district offices spread out under the various regional offices. The districts are headed by a district director. The people in the district offices are the ones who come in contact with the public. These are the folks you meet when you go in for an audit.

These are the folks who seize your business or assets and drag you out of your car if they want to seize it. These are the ones who go to your office to audit your books. Their basic tax collecting divisions are the Collection Division and the Taxpayer Service Division. They also have basic support organizations like the regional offices and the National offices. The districts only function is to collect taxes.

Service Centers. The IRS has ten service centers. The service centers are comparable to a district office. They report directly to a regional office. They are headed by a service center director. Their job is to process tax returns and related documents. They do not deal with the public face to face.

The IRS Takes a Token

I should start this with, "It was a dark and rainy night..." But this is not fiction. At times it might sound like it. Nor was it dark and rainy when I fell in with the Internal Revenue Service. It was a bright sunny day. I was relaxing in my office in Alameda, California, watching a couple of sailboats meandering down the estuary between Alameda and Oakland. The phone rang. It was the chief of the personnel branch.

She said, "Oscar, we just got a job announcement in from the IRS. They want someone to head their new Finance Office in Fresno, California. The announcement qualifications read like they were looking for you."

I asked, "What is the IRS doing in Fresno?"

"I don't know, "she said. "The announcement says something about a new service center. Are you interested?"

"I don't know," I replied. "I don't know anything about the IRS."

She said, "Let's go to lunch and I'll bring the announcement with me."

I studied it during lunch. It made me curious, I went back to my office and called the IRS's personnel office in San Francisco. They told me the IRS was building a new service center in Fresno, California to process tax returns.

It would be like the one in Ogden, Utah which was processing tax returns for the West Coast.

I thought about the job for a couple of days. I didn't know any more about the IRS than the average taxpayer. My general feeling about the IRS was negative. But I liked change. I talked it over with my wife and decided to submit an application for the job.

A number of weeks went by and out of the blue, the IRS called me. They wanted me to come in for an interview. There were to be two interviews of the top five candidates. One would be an individual interview with three IRS officials and the second would be a group interview. I chuckled to myself because I had just finished reading a management book which had recently been published dealing with group interviews. I thought this would be a good chance to practice the techniques.

The first interview was conducted by the Assistant Regional Commissioner for Human Resources, the Regional Fiscal management Officer, and the new Chief of the Human Resources Division of the Fresno Service Center. The interview went well. One of them made an observation that I changed jobs often. He was looking at my resume. It showed that I had worked all over the country in ten different jobs in the twenty years that I had worked for the Department of Defense.

He asked, "If you were selected, how long would you stay with the IRS?" I told him, "I guarantee you two years, one year to get the financial office up and running and a second year to see that it ran smoothly." I told them I changed jobs on an average of every two years because I got bored easily and a number of theses job changes in fact were situations where I started new offices from scratch. I said, "I am looking forward to an opportunity to develop the Finance Office in Fresno." I couldn't read any particular body language of the interviewers in response to what I had said. I felt some discomfort in dealing with the question because I thought they might be looking at me as a job hopper, i.e., someone who jumps from job to job and never finishes anything.

When we were introduced at the beginning of the group interview, I found that two of the interviewees were IRS employees.I had a lot of fun in the second interview. I played the game right by the book I had just read on how to win in group interviews. I made myself the chairman of the group by addressing each person, asking for their input on the question the panel had given us to work on. I limited the time the other participants talked by directing questions to the other candidates when I thought the person had talked long enough. I ended the interview by summarizing our findings. I could feel the frustration building in the other interviewees as the group interview progressed. Their glances, shifting in their chairs told me I was winning the game.

I was not too surprised when I got a call from the IRS offering me the job. I knew I had aced the interviews. Our new offices were not ready in Fresno, so I worked in the regional office in San Francisco for three months. This gave me time to familiarize myself with IRS policies and practices and the time to sit up the procedures for my new office. It also gave me an opportunity to meet and interact with the various offices in the Regional Headquarters. I learned long ago that a little PR can go a long way. However, I was a little taken back when I walked into the Budget

Office. The two IRS employees who were interviewed with me for the job I got worked in this office. They were both senior budget analysts. I had a need to go into the Budget Office frequently to research reference material or discuss some of the budget issues with the analyst. Walking into that office was like walking into a cold storage locker. When I walked into the office, all conversation stopped. Everyone seemed to have something important to work on at their desk. I concluded that everyone in the office was a bunch of poor losers. I made it a point to be as unfriendly as they were toward me. I asked specific questions concerning budget issues. They reluctantly responded to my questions. I was quick to give a sarcastic, "Thank you."

During this same time, I made a number of trips to the Ogden Utah Service Center. My counterpart there was a gruff, old loner. I realized he liked his distance and did not try to establish any rapport with him. He let me use his office to confer with the employees who were slated to move to Fresno. I advised them on what they could expect in reimbursement for moving expenses and the pitfalls they could incur if they didn't maintain correct documentation. One day I was sitting in his office waiting for the next client to show up when out of the blue, he said, "You know they don't like you in the (regional) budget office. They think one of their people should have gotten the job."

I replied, "I know that."

He said, "I was just letting you know what they think about you."

I said, "What do you think about one of their people not getting the job?"

He replied, "I don't care anything about those people. I didn't care who got the job."

I believed him. I had already developed an opinion that he didn't care much for the people in the Region. In fact I had concluded he didn't care much for anyone. After that sort of ice breaking conversation we struck up a kind of comradery. In a sense we were both sort of undesirables when it came to the people in the Budget Office in the Regional Office. He told me about his passion for visiting and collecting license plates from every state in the Union. He still had about twelve to go. He planned to retire within a couple of years and collect the remaining twelve plates.

The one thing that surprised me more than ever about this guy was the fact he was not a Mormon. At least ninety percent of the people who work in the Ogden Utah Service Center are Mormon. Not only was he not Mormon but he demonstrated an open disdain for the religion. The first time I saw this I was shocked. Someone said something about, "The Church," My counterpart started mumbling all kinds of invectives under his breath about the church and, "Those damn Mormon." I couldn't believe that he could be working there in the job he was in with that openly hostile attitude. I found out later that he didn't voluntarily go to Ogden. He was a transplant from the old payroll center. Over the next couple of years I developed a respect for him. He reminded me a lot of the first instructor I had when I took flying lessons. His gruff exterior kept people at a distance, but if he let you past his defense system you found an amenable, cooperative, friendly but guarded person.

We finally moved into our permanent building in Fresno. I was glade to get out of the cramped temporary office I had been in for months. Arthur Murry made the building a dance studio after our departure. I was busy as could be hiring and training the remainder of my staff. Around me the organization began to fill up. As I watched the organization fill up a cold reality began to enter my consciousness. I was one black face among a sea of white faces. I didn't want to admit it to myself. I finally had to face the truth. I had been hired as a token black. I looked back at the interview and remembered one of the statements one of the interviewers made during the job interview. He said, "I see you have changed jobs often." Common sense now told me this staid, old-fashioned organization would not have hired a job hopper like me over two of their own qualified loyal employees. I didn't beat out the two IRS budget analysts with whom I competed for my job. They didn't get the job because they were the wrong color. They were white. My enthusiasm for the job and the organization began to wain.

I was upset by my realization, but I didn't have a lot of time to dwell on it. That would come later. I had to get my new office going. I had to hire and train my staff. The duties of my office included budget preparation and execution; payroll/timekeeping; travel voucher examination; vendor invoice processing; and doing management analysis studies. Later I added the responsibility of the Quality review program for the, Mail-out Program. I had to start hiring and training people right away in order to get going in the areas of payroll, timekeeping, and travel reimbursement. There were people coming in every day who needed assistance in these areas.

Payroll in the Renaissance

All federal offices, except for the IRS paid their employees every other week on Friday. The IRS pays its employees on Monday. I never could get what I consider to be a totally rational answer for this. I talked to the people in the payroll center in Detroit, Michigan. I talked to people in our regional office in San Francisco and the National Office in Washington, D.C. The answers were varied. The answer I finally settled upon was that it gave the payroll center two extra days, i.e., Saturday and Sunday, to process the payroll. They really didn't need those two days but they were there in case something happened. My gut level feeling is that for some bizarre reason long ago something traumatic happened. Today no one remembers what happened but no one wants to change the IRS payday to conform to the rest of the federal government.

This payday thing may seem trivial but it had an effect on our employees when they saw all other federal workers getting their paychecks on Friday, three days before they got theirs. A small number of the employees figured out a system which worked sometime to get around the Monday payday, and get their checks earlier. They discovered that if they had their checks mailed to their home, it often arrived on Friday. If it didn't come in on Friday there was the chance, it would come in on Saturday. Every other Friday there was a conspicuous exodus of people going home to check their mail. The checks were dated for Monday. This didn't stop them from cashing them or depositing them into their bank account. If it wasn't there on Friday, some people were so disgruntled they called my office to complain. My people reminded them that Monday was payday. Sometimes these smart people got out smarted and their checks didn't arrive at their home until Monday or later.

The distribution of checks was done in my office. A mail carrier went to the post office on Monday and brought three large boxes of checks to my office. My people went through the checks, pulled some for various reasons such as employee indebtedness to the IRS, incorrect amount, the employee was on leave, etc. The remaining checks were batched according to branch. After a furious number of hours of sorting checks, and telling people on the phone, "Yes the checks were here but not ready yet," my payroll coordinator called each branch and told them when to pick up their checks. The branches distributed the checks to their employees. I had not seen a system like this for at least ten years. All of the previous agencies I worked for required you to either have your checks mailed to your home or went via direct deposit to your bank. Imagine the disruption of work during check distribution, when we reached our peak of over six thousand employees. People leaving the complex at noon to deposit their checks in their bank or cash them, made the parking lot look like the Los Angeles freeway during commute hours. I immediately began to push for full home mail or direct deposit. My pleas fell on deaf ears, as would happen later when I was pushing for centralized timekeeping and time clocks.

On one Monday payday, my payroll coordinator and the mail courier came into my office. The courier said the words I never wanted to hear. "The checks were not at the post office." I told the courier to go back and stay there until they came, or I called him with other instructions. I called our payroll center in Detroit. I was assured the payroll tapes went out on Thursday to the San Francisco Disbursing Center. The disbursing center is the office which prints the checks and mails them to various offices and to those who receive their mail at home. I called the disbursing center. They assured me the checks were mailed out on Friday. I called the Regional Fiscal Management Officer (RFMO) in San Francisco. I told him we had a little problem.

We discussed the options available to us which were: (1) wait and hope the checks showed up, or (2) have the disbursing center run a complete new set of checks and we would send someone up to San Francisco to pick them up. I discussed this with my division chief and we agreed the only safe option was to rerun the checks. I called our San Francisco office and told them to have the disbursing center run a full set of new checks.

About two thirty that afternoon, the mail courier called from the post office. The boxes of checks had been found sitting outside on the loading ramp at the post office. It didn't make any difference at this point, now that the checks were found, but it was obvious a postal employee had mistakenly taken the checks on his route. After discovering them he probably discretely placed them on the outside loading dock and disappeared. I told the courier to open the boxes and see what was inside. He said that they were full of checks. He started for the center immediately. I called the regional office and told them to stop the Disbursing Center reprint. They were over half way through the reprint. The reprinted checks had to be destroyed. We were very late getting the checks out to the branches for distribution. At that time we had about four thousand people. They were milling around the Center for hours waiting for us to get the checks distributed. Our phones had been ringing so much we took them off of the hooks. Even though the IRS was responsible for these people staying after their work hours to receive their checks, they were not compensated.

After this fiasco, I pushed harder for mandatory home mail or direct deposit for all employees' earnings. Management continued to ignore me. After all, this is the way it always was, why change? In 1975 the payroll center in Detroit planned to change to a new computer system. I had been through major computer changes twice before in other agencies. The smart agency ran a parallel system until all of the bugs were worked out. The not so smart agency, trying to save a few nickels, went on line with their new system at the same time that they took their old system off line. Within a few weeks the not so smart agency had such a mess on their hands that they had to take the new system down and revert to manual processing. The chief of the Computer Services Division was fired.

I called our payroll center and asked if they were going to run parallel systems. They informed me they had no choice. The National Office had said they would not run parallel systems. I didn't want to hear that. After the third payday under the new system, the payroll program had turned to chaos. Our office developed an inventory of over thirteen hundred payroll problems. This amounted to over one fourth of our work force. There were hundreds of people who got no pay or were underpaid. I issued emergency salary advances to those who received no pay or significantly less than they should have. This compounded the problem because now each of their accounts had to have another adjustment. Some people had pay errors in multiple pay periods. Every office in the IRS was going through this. Imagine what a morale problem we had. When people are not paid correctly, they don't work effectively. The supervisors kept my phones ringing. I thought of retiring but I was too young.

I was trying to develop a coherent plan of action. I went to our payroll center in Detroit, Michigan. They were up to their eyeballs in alligators. Crying on their shoulders wouldn't have helped us. I made an agreement with the managers at the center. They would train one of my people in their process of making account adjustments. I would set up a task force at the center. My person would train them and oversee their work. We would do all of the research and using their forms get everything ready for input into the computer. Their people would simply review it before input.

I went back to Fresno and sent one of my employee for training. After she returned to Fresno, she selected the people for our task force and started their training. These things don't just happen overnight. Even though we were paddling as fast as we could we were not yet making any headway against the current of payroll problems. During this period, in which I was trying to get things moving in the right direction we got a new assistant director for the service center. His name was Gary Mathews. To me his actions mimicked what we called in the service a new shave tail lieutenant, still wet behind the ears. Almost every day, my division chief came to me saying the assistant director wanted me to do this or that. I ignored his suggestions. His passing down of commands became more persistent. I finally got fed up with his constant barrage of directions through my division chief to me. I wrote the assistant direct a memorandum. It read;

To:	Assistant Director
Through:	Chief Human Resources Division
Subject:	Payroll Problem Resolution

We have a serious payroll problem. I have taken steps to resolve our problem. It will not happen overnight.

The directions you are sending to me through the chief of the Human Resources Division are not helping me solve the payroll problems. In fact, they are slowing me down.

I think it is time we had a blood letting.

Fiscal Officer
Oscar Williams

I know this sounds overly dramatic. In fact it sounds like plain old hokey, but that was how I felt at that moment. When my division chief got the memo he called me and asked, "Do you really want me to send this forward?"

I responded, "I sure do." He had his secretary hand carry it to the assistant director's office. Within a half hour, I got a call from the assistant director.

He said, "I got your memo. When do you want to meet?"

I said, "How about four o'clock in the director's conference room?"

He said, "Be there," and hung up.

I called my division chief and told him about the meeting. He asked, "Do you mind if I sit in?" I said, "I think you should." This was Harvey Kuffner, my first of three division chiefs. He was the smart one who left the IRS and started a successful computer consulting service.

When I got to the conference room, the assistant director and my division chief were there. As soon as I sat down, the assistant director went into a tyrannical ranting about how he was the assistant director and he can become involved in any program in the center that he chose to.

I had anticipated this. I had taken into consideration the fact he was young, inexperienced and used to the IRS way which meant subordinates didn't talk back. When he finally stopped for breath, I told him that he got paid to be the assistant director, not the fiscal officer. If he was going to do my job, then he should get both of our pay. He jumped in with another barrage.

When he stopped for breath again, I proceeded to tell him what I was doing to resolve the problems. I said, "I am doing all that is humanly possible to clean up our mess." While I had his attention, I continued on and told him my plans which had been put into motion to resolve the mess. I ended my point by saying, "I want you to stay out of my business until I have had time to get things under control. Don't send me messages about what I should be doing. If you are not satisfied with my work, remove me from my job and put someone else in there." The three of us sat there looking at each other. My division chief, Harvey Kuffner had not said anything. He was not afraid of getting into the fray. I think he was enjoying watching the proceedings.

The assistant director was getting control of himself. In a low firm voice he said, "I'll give you time to get things cleaned up. If I don't see improvement, I will replace you." We sat there for a moment in strained silence. Mathews left the room. My division chief said, "For a while there, I wasn't sure how things would turn out." I said, "I think it was nip and tuck for a while." By hindsight I realized I could have handled the situation with more diplomacy. I could have asked for a meeting with the assistant director, outlined my plan for him, and asked for his blessing. The truth was, I needed someone to yell at. I couldn't yell at my employees. I couldn't yell at the thirteen hundred employees with payroll problems. But at times I did raise my voice during the exchange with the Assistant director. I felt much better after our meeting.

Sandra Swabie, my assistant did an excellent job training the payroll cadre.

As soon as the training was finished, they tackled the horrendous payroll mess we had on our hands. I had the task force set up in a training room. Much of their time was spent researching; reconstructing payroll records; and making adjustments. They also had to have meetings with employees to verify data and ensure the problems were completely resolved. I was proud of the work the task force did. We got a number of complements from the payroll center on the thoroughness of the paper work which was sent to them.

Below is a picture of my task force. On the far right is my assistant Sandra Schwabie. The lady on the left, front row, Rachel Hunsaker eventually became my full time payroll coordinator.

In about two months we had pretty well cleaned up the backlog. I disbanded my task force and my people began working on the residual of overpaid cases. A number of people had told us about their overpayment and we had made adjustments. The payroll center had caught up and was now identifying people who had been paid double from one to three pay periods and had not told us. Invariably the employees claimed they didn't realize what had happened. It is not possible for a person to get up to double their pay and not notice it. I believe they saw the mess we had and took a calculated gamble that they would not be caught. I had no sympathy for those people. What made the cheese more binding was we were nearing the end of the tax year. They came crying to me about having to pay taxes on money which wasn't theirs. I just smiled and said, "You know the tax laws."

The IRS finally started to catch up to the rest of the world. They began serious consideration of moving toward home mail and direct deposit. This was not done in one fell swoop. A concentrated public relations program was initiated to get employees to sign up for these programs. The weak point of the programs was, **enrollment was voluntary**. We ended up with three almost equally divided systems, i.e., receive their check at the office, at home, or direct deposit.

There were glitches in our direct deposit system which began to show up soon after we started the system. Large banks were sent one lump sum of money VIA an electronic transfer of funds from the San Francisco Disbursing Center. A tape listing the employees, their account numbers, and the amount of money which was to be deposited to their account, was sent from our payroll center. Smaller banks received an individual check for the few employees they might have. The large banks' centralized processing centers were having trouble associating the lump sum they received with the people listed on the tape. This led to the employees accounts being posted late in the various branches. The small banks were claiming they were late getting our employees checks or in some cases they claimed the checks were never received.

People had checks bouncing all over the place. Believe it or not, people do write checks in anticipation of their account being credited. The employees were being charged for bounced checks and they were mad. The employees and their supervisors were calling and coming up to my office in droves. I thought about retiring again. I was still too young. I tried to get some type of organized chaos comingled with the absolute chaos which was going on. I had each branch make a list of the people who had not been paid and whether or not they had bounced checks.

I had my most diplomatic employee call each of the banks explaining that we had problems and asked them to wave the bounced check fees. I was surprised when all of the banks agreed. My employee even had to call some landlords to stop them from hassling our employees over bounced rent checks. I have no idea what this did to some employees' credit. At the same time we were dealing with the banks and landlords, we were issuing emergency salary advances to tide the employees over. We had a replacement checks issued which arrived at our office within three of four days from the time we ordered them. This meant the employee got a check about three days after they discovered that their checks had bounced. This could be weeks from the time they should have been paid. All of that public relations was wasted. The employees began canceling their direct deposit accounts en masse. We were basically back where we started. At least the home mail system seemed to be going okay. "Ha!"

One pay period we began getting calls from all over the center. Employees claimed they had not received their check at home. This was the Friday before payday. My people gave them the standard answer, "Payday was Monday. Go away." Monday rolled around and droves of people went home to check their mail. Soon our phones were tied up with people complaining that their mail had arrived but not their check. I called the Disbursing Center in San Francisco. They said the checks went out on Thursday.

I called the local post office. They did not know of any problems in the postal system. I put the word out throughout the center that we would just have to wait for the checks to come through the mail. Another day went bye. We almost had a riot on our hands. I remembered that I had thirty-two thousand dollars in my safe. I usually kept about two thousand for small purchases. I had obtained the extra thirty thousand for a special project. The project had not started. I decided to set up an old fashioned army payroll station.

I had my people hand carry a memo to each branch explaining how they were to get their employees to fill out the paperwork and telling them what time they were to bring their people to a large training room where I had set up a payroll station. We gave some cash to those who had to have some money immediately. We ordered emergency salary checks for those who could wait three days. Watching the people coming in signing; for their money; and counting it before they left the table, took me back to when I was in uniform during the Korean War. I wondered how much further our payroll system could regress.

The missing checks began to be delivered back to the Disbursing Center in San Francisco. Someone finally realized what had happened. The disbursing center had used envelopes which allowed the employee's social security number to show through the clear plastic window. The postal mail sorting machine was reading the social security number as the zip code and sent the checks all over the country. This news did not stop our employees from canceling their home mail. We found ourselves back in the business of handing out over five thousand checks within the center, every other week. During the interview for my position, I was told the selectee would be responsible for timekeeping. I envisioned what I had experienced for the previous twenty years of my career. I assumed that every two weeks, my people would have new time cards punched up, put them in the racks, pick up the old time cards, make adjustments to tours, i.e., annual leave, sick leave, and over-time. They would reconcile any problems with the appropriate supervisor, punch the information into the card, and send it in for payroll processing.

This was not to be. Walking into the IRS was like walking way back in time. Timekeeping was done manually by part time timekeepers. I had never seen or heard of manual timekeeping in a major sized organization. There are situations where a manual system is dictated. Stevedores, people whom load ships use a manual system of time keeping because the people manning the crews changed constantly, from day to day and ship to ship. When I was in New York in contract administration, we had seven people in the office. Work time was kept manually. This made sense with seven people, but when our IRS organization reached its full compliment of six thousand employees, I would have over two hundred part time time-keepers scattered throughout the service center manually recording employees work time on scrapes of paper. All of our employees were in our personal system. It would have been so simple to print time cards for each employee; place them in racks; have the employees punch in and out each day; pick the cards up at the end of the two week pay period; and send the data to the payroll center in Detroit.

There I sat, in disbelief with two hundred part time timekeepers scattered over twelve acres of buildings. One hundred of them were primary timekeepers and the other one hundred were backups, to fill in the absence of the primary or to assist because of the fluctuating workload. I had to get these people designated; trained; oversaw their daily functions; and ensure that the information was sent to our payroll processing center in Detroit in a timely manner. I couldn't vouch for the quality of what was sent to the payroll center. I didn't even know what we sent to the payroll center in Detroit most of the time.

The timekeepers were clerks and secretaries. Some of them were sharp. Many of them couldn't find their way to the bathroom. The reason for this was the average supervisor didn't want their best producers being pulled off of production to be trained and to do timekeeping functions. The turnover was horrendous. As soon as a timekeeper was trained, he or she was promoted to some other area and a new person had to be trained to take their place. Just like any organization, we had changes in regulations. This required keeping all two hundred of them abreast of the changes. Because of all of these factors, the number of errors were astronomical. No one seemed to be bothered by the amount of errors being made, because this was the way it had always been.

One of my staff people did the training and coordination with the timekeepers. Even though I was not involved in the daily operation of the time keeping system it still took a large amount of my time dealing with the problems it created. As soon as I saw the situation, I started pushing to have us go to a time clock system. With a time clock system,

I could do the job with five full time people. Another alternative I tried was to get approval to set up a small permanent staff of timekeepers in my office. Each time, I was told our national office in Washington, D.C. wouldn't buy into this idea. I doubt very much if my proposals ever got to the national office.

In the mid-seventies, I heard a rumor that one of our service centers had developed a centralized timekeeping system. I called the service center in Memphis, Tennessee. The chief of the Human Resources Division told me he had established a centralized system and it was working well. I asked him if I could take a look at it. He said, "Sure, y'all come on down anytime you want to." I was on the plane to Memphis the following week.

The first question I asked the division chief was how did he get National Office approval. His reply was, "Ah don't even know if the National Office knows we have it." I was astonished. I asked him on what authority his director had approved his plan. He said, "He don't need no approval, he's got big balls." Obviously his director came from outside of the IRS. He went on to say, "When I convinced him that we could reduce payroll problems by centralizing, he said to do it." I knew then that I was skating on thin ice. I had worked for three directors. They were all men and only one of them had balls and he had a nervous breakdown. I liked what I saw. A small group of well trained people doing a high quality job.

On the way back to Fresno, I pondered over the question, "How can I sell the centralized concept?" It was obvious that I didn't need national office approval. I needed a director with balls. I didn't have one. I decided to try a softer approach. When I got back to Fresno, I pulled out my old worn proposal for centralization of time keeping. I dusted it off and inserted some junk about running a test of the centralization concept in two branches and comparing the error rate to the other ten branches. I proposed going with the most accurate system of the two systems. The director agonized for days over this. Finally he gave the approval for the test. There was no way it could fail. After all, I was the one developing the statistics. Even if I had not been watching so closely any system would have reduced errors over the current decentralized system.

After the three-month test, the other branches were clamoring for the system centralized system. They realized that with the centralized system, their involvement was reduced to a minimum and they were convinced the system reduced errors which gave them fewer problems. An employee with a payroll problem is not performing at his peak. We implemented centralized throughout the center. I selected a supervisor for the unit who in turn hired a payroll coordinator and sixteen timekeepers. I reduced my two hundred timekeepers to eighteen full time people.

Oh, yes, the payroll coordinator. That was not part of the original deal, nor did Memphis have one. I thought this was a good time to sneak a full time coordinator in rather than have one of my immediate staff doing those duties. What's one more body? I had my timekeeping supervisor provide me with an error rate report each pay period. The error rate plummeted and remained at an insignificant level. The idea spread throughout the large offices in the nation. Five years later, the National Office came out with instructions for centralizing timekeeping. The option was left up to each director to remain decentralized or go centralized. By then most large offices had made the change. Could this be a case of the tail wagging the dog?

When I left the IRS after being with them for seventeen years, with the exception of centralized timekeeping, nothing in the timekeeping and payroll systems had changed. It was etched in stone, "This is the way it has always been and this is the way it will stay!"

Equal Employment Opportunity

Equal employment opportunity (EEO) is a term which has become synonymous with affirmative action in some walks of life because some people don't know the difference. Equal employment opportunity in its simplest terms is providing equal access to qualified people to compete for jobs, developmental assignments and training. Affirmative action requires that preferences be made to minorities and women in filling jobs; providing training; promotions; and details. Under EEO there is a basic need to put in place a system, which provides equal access for jobs to all people, provide a process for review and a system of making a person whole who has been denied an opportunity to compete on a level playing field. There is no provision for preferences under a true EEO system.

The three problems, which the Internal Revenue Service created within its EEO program, is a lack of understanding of the basic requirements, a lack of commitment on the part of the IRS's managers and a defensive punitive attitude toward any employee who makes a claim of discrimination and asked to be made whole. The following personal experiences I encountered within the IRS illustrates the weaknesses in the policies and practices of the IRS's EEO program.

The Token Turns

As my tenure continued with the IRS, it became apparent I was correct in my assumption that they had bought me as a token to add some color to the organization. I saw that we had no minority seeds in the organization who were being developed for advancement. I call seeds people who are in career ladders at lower grades who are being groomed to move up in the organization. There were none in the Regional Office. None in the Fresno Service Center, and for sure, there were none in the Ogden (Utah) Service Center.

The Fresno Service Center could not buy enough black, brown, red, and yellow employees to fill in the voids their Equal Employment Opportunity System created. Because there was no system in place to ensure minorities were being given an equal opportunity to compete for promotions; training; and details the situation within the Center had became quite abysmal for minorities. In 1976 twelve-minority managers and supervisors at the Center formed an EEO Ad Hoc Committee. There was a total of seventeen minority managers and supervisors. Five chose not to join the group. At that time the center had over four thousand people and we were growing every day toward a peak of over six thousand. I was a member the Ad Hoc Committee. I was the highest graded manager in the group.

We did not invite non supervisory people to join us because we did not want to place them in jeopardy. We felt that as managers and supervisors, we could protect ourselves from any management harassment. Our purpose was to address the wide spread problems we saw in minorities

being systematically excluded from developmental assignments, promotions, and a general disparity of minorities at
all significant administrative and management levels. There
were two branches we coined, "The Twin Temples" because
the branch chiefs were Mormon and all of the managers and
supervisors they hired or promoted were Mormon, male and
white. This was 1976. It was not until 1978 that the leader
of the Mormon Church met with God and God decreed
that blacks were okay and could now be allowed to ascend
to the higher levels of the church. Even though the Mormon
church allegedly changed its practices to this day, they still
have a written doctrine of discrimination. Our group felt
there was clear statistical evidence that the Mormon doctrine
was being carried into the work place in the two branches
we called, "The twin temples."

We developed a data base consisting of promotions,
developmental training and details. Inasmuch as we were
dispersed throughout the center, it was easy to document
the processes which concerned us. After developing and
analyzing our package, we prepared a report. We asked for
and got a meeting with the director. We reviewed the
package with him. After the review and some discussion we
asked him to make a commitment to us to deal with what
we considered blatant discriminatory practices.

The director was a good politician and would make not
make any type of commitment. He told us he would have
his division chiefs study the package and would get back
to us. Talk about asking the fox to watch the chickens.
These practices had been going on for years in all divisions
and he was going to have the foxes who created and perpet-
uated the situation, study the chicken's package.

We were not surprised by the director's conclusion. He met with us a second time, and informed us that his staff had concluded there was no validity to our claim. Hence no action was going to be taken. Knowing how the IRS managers mind works, we had not been just sitting around waiting for a response from the director. We had anticipated his response and had already begun drafting a letter to the regional commissioner in San Francisco. After our second meeting with the director we finalized the letter and sent it off. About two weeks later we received a letter from the regional commissioner informing us that he was going to send a special Equal Opportunity (EEO) investigator to the center to look into our allegations. We were satisfied with this action because an EEO investigator's job is to get the facts and present them in an analytical and objective manner. This was the most objective review which could be made within the agency. The investigator finished the job and gave his report to the regional commissioner. Normally complainants are given a copy of an investigator's report. We were not given a copy of the report or allowed to see the report.

When I worked in the regional office for three months, I spent a lot of time getting to know people, one on one. I used one of these contacts in the Equal Employment Opportunity Office to find out what was in the report. He said, "I can't tell you all of the details but let me just say that all of your allegations were supported and the regional commissioner is furious." He told me to wait for some significant action. I passed this on to our group. We waited.

The only thing the IRS fears is exposure by the media. I had not shared with the group the fact that I had a contingency plan. I had contacted a local black newsman. I showed him the package we had sent to the regional commissioner. After he reviewed the material, he was ready to go to press immediately. After some negotiation we made an agreement that if the regional commissioner did not act on our complaint, he would publish it in its entirety. I told the newsman about my discussion with my inside source in the Region. Our agreement was that he wait to see what the response would be from the regional commissioner. The newsman must have got tired of waiting. Without discussing it with me the reporter called the Service Center Director, Fred Perdue. He wanted to get Perdue's reaction to our charges.

After the call the director came storming into my office and threw himself into one of my chairs. My division chief was in my office. He had dropped by to talk about some finance issue. The director said, "Some newsman just called me. I didn't know what the hell he was talking about. Who the hell is Mr. Charlie?" For a moment I thought my cover was blown. I thought the director was in my office because the newsman had given him my name. I am lucky that at times I know when to keep my mouth shut. I soon realized that the director was directing his speech to my division chief. Apparently my division chief's secretary had told the director that he was in my office.

I knew that the director had talked to the newsman because I had told the newsman, "The IRS measured its EEO accomplishments by numbers. It just so happens that most of the minorities are the big numbers at the bottom of the heap. If we measured Mr. Charlie's EEO, accomplishments in the same way he would be a leader in EEO."

The newsman knew what I meant because he is black. The director had no idea that Mr. Charlie was a reference to a hypothetical white slave owner. African Americans use the term Mr. Charlie to depict a white person whom they consider to be a bigot. As soon as the director left my office I called the newsman and told him his phone call had shaken up the director. I told him I was glad he had created a little bit of frustration on the part of the director to match some of the frustration felt by the Ad Hoc Committee. However, I had to ask him to hold off taking any more action until I gave him the go ahead. He agreed.

The EEO Ad Hoc Committee received a letter from the regional commissioner dated May 24, 1977. It read and I quote:

Dear Committee:

I have recently received the investigation file from Mr. Hector Mazon concerning the allegations as stated in your February 22, 1977-letter.

After carefully reviewing this report, I feel there is a need to enhance our EEO program and to assess the limited achievements at the Fresno Service Center. While these efforts will be intensified, I want to assure you that EEO is a viable part of the IRS mission. Dedication to these principles is a high priority in the Western Region. In addition, I feel we have made significant progress in addressing the EEO concerns of women and minorities in several areas; however, we still need a concerted effort from every manager if we are to achieve success.

I am confident that you will note a more positive and results oriented EEO program in the next
few months.

> Sincerely,
> Thomas A. Cardoza
> Regional Commissioner

End quote. Some people might not be used to bureaucratic double talk. This letter basically said the managers
in Fresno were negligent; were not doing their jobs; and he
was going to kick some butt. Soon after we received the
letter from the regional commissioner, the director asked
for a meeting with our group. He told us he had recon-
sidered his position concerning our complaints. He didn't
mention our letter to the regional commissioner, the EEO
investigator, or the results of the investigation. He told us
that he and his staff had drawn up an action plan to overcome the problems noted in our package. This was a strange
turn about. Just six months ago, the director told us his staff
had determined that there was no validity to our claims.
Now he and the same group were developing a plan to
overcome those nonexistent problems. Isn't this a classical
example of schizophrenia?

There was a whirlwind of activity. Minorities were
appointed to committees, developmental programs and
other places where they could be seen. Some employees
were being developed against their will. One of the women
on our Ad Hoc Committee was selected for training she
didn't want. This whirlwind of activity did not resolve the
major problems which were the IRS had an equal employment opportunity program on paper only. It was not an

ongoing part of management philosophy and practice and programs were not in place to ensure EEO considerations. The director and his staff were dealing with the symptoms of the problem in trying to correct a condition overnight which took years to develop. From my perspective it was disgusting to watch what was happening. It was not what the Committee envisioned. We envisioned a systematic process of analysis, training and assessment. I guess the actions the director took was better than nothing. But this kind of problem solving has no lasting effect.

We disbanded our Ad Hoc Committee. We agreed that we would watch what was happening over the long term. If we saw the situation deteriorate we would act. I called the newsman and told him not to publish the story.

I would like to express my congratulations to the minority managers and supervisors who put themselves on the firing line to thwart the racism being fostered at the Fresno Service Center, Fresno, California. They stemmed the tide. Those, who followed in their footsteps, do not realize how much the actions of this group affected their future. The EEO Ad Hoc Committee members were:

Eddie Mae Washington   Chris Sanchez
Ray Reyes   Jose Valdez
Frank Pantoya   Oscar Williams
Mary Chavis
Millie Byrd
Alfred Burley
Simon Sauceda
Josie Hyre
Johnnie reed

Back to the Future

It would seem from the preceding that the director and his staff had got the picture. Wrong! They fell back into their old habits. Many service centers had night managers during the peak production period. The position acts basically as the night director. The person in this position didn't set policy or practices. He was simply the focal point of communication on the swing shift. One of the night branch chiefs could have simply carried out the duties of night manager. However, the director and his staff decided they wanted a night manager. This job provided a good opportunity for an up and coming manager to get some good brownie points for their resume.

The only problem with the decision to have a night manager was the method the director and his staff chose to fill the position. Two years in a row, the good old boys selected a good old white boy. The director and his staff (his division chiefs) met and through some kind of popularity contest the division chiefs nominated people from their respective divisions to fill the night manager position. After the nominations they then voted on who would be selected.

I saw some serious problems with the process the director and his staff used to select the night manager. The key two problems I had with their process of selection were in the first two years of their selection process black people were not considered and secondly the position was not made competitive so that the job requirements would be defined and any qualified person could apply. In the most simple terms there was no consideration for providing a level playing field for competition. The most basic EEO fundamental concept. I thought about the situation and decided their good old boy's method of selecting the night manager was unacceptable. I wrote a memorandum to my division chief, Bob Maddux, pointing out that the system the director and his staff were using to select the night manager was excluding many people. I suggested that the position be announced competitively each year so that all qualified employees would have the opportunity to be considered.

I was ignored, of course. Knowing Bob as I did, I had no doubt that he would not take my concerns to the director or the other staff members. In January of 1980, I filled an EEO complaint. My complaint stated, "blacks were systematically excluded from the opportunity to be considered for the position of night manager because of the clandestine method used by the director and his staff in filling the position."

Because of the grade of the position, there were only two blacks in the whole service center of six thousand people who could be considered to fill the position. Those two were the statistician and myself. I was the only black manager. An Equal Employment Opportunity investigator was assigned to my case. During the investigation he placed our director, Theron Polivka and each of his staff under oath and questioned them as to their objectives and methodology in filling the position. Watching them squirm and grasp for cover did my heart good. It was like watching a bunch of grubs running from the sunlight after you raise up an old decaying log. The crux of the questioning centered around two issues. The issues were: Why weren't the only two qualified Blacks in the center considered and why were qualifications now being required which previous white appointees did not have? A lot of their testimony would fit well in a script for one of Abbott and Costello's Comedy movies. Some of the excerpts from their testimony follow:

Three of the division chiefs didn't remember my name being mentioned during the process. Three of them and the director remembered my name being mentioned. (However, there was no record of my name being mentioned in the director's secretaries notes).

One division chief said she remembers the statistician being nominated for the job. Her division chief said he did not nominate her because she was in a one of a kind position. Later he changed his testimony and said he did not nominate her because she needed more development.

The director said, "I do not remember Equal Employment Opportunity being mentioned, but I am committed to the EEO objectives of the Service Center and EEO is inherent in any selection made." End quote.

The director's statement that EEO is inherent in any selection made really left me wondering which dictionary he used to define, inherent. Inherent to me means something is basically a part of something or a process. Based upon his statement, isn't it reasonable to assume that sometime during the process of identifying and selecting a good old white boy, this inherent process of EEO would have cut in and automatically qualified minorities would have been considered equally for the position. My gut level feeling is this inherent consideration only surfaced after I filed my complaint.

The investigator asked them why they had not used the position description as their criteria for appointment. Their response was, no one knew a position description existed for the job. They didn't know that it was an administrative job, not a technical job. The job was classified in April of 1979. I obtained a copy of the job description before I filed my complaint. I wanted to be sure that I qualified for the position.

In filling the position the director and his staff made up quasi qualifications for the job as they went along. These qualifications were structured to meet the experience of the person they selected. The investigator asked them why a white section chief in the same division I was in, who did not meet their (made up) criteria for the job, was appointed. **No one remembered why**. Those eight very high paid civil servants appointed that man, using some kind of criteria. Not one of them remembered what the criteria were. These are the people paid to manage the organization whose memory had suddenly dissipated. I believe that the investigator's following summary puts their actions in the proper perspective. I quote:

"The position description for the night shift manager does not require computer experience and tends to support Oscar Williams' allegation that this experience was used to justify appointing the present night manager instead of Oscar because he had no computer experience.

There appears to be an inconsistent method used to select the night manager when in the previous year, computer and pipeline experience was not strongly emphasized.

The position description does not require any technical knowledge and appears to be an administrative position." End quote.

The investigator's summary described how the director and his division chiefs, the highest paid people and supposedly the best minds in the organization, had made decisions based upon hearsay and some kind of hidden agenda. Collectively they didn't even have enough knowledge of the system to ever think the job in question had been classified and had a job description. Not having a job description didn't stop them from making up a description which fitted the qualifications of the, good old white boy, they wanted to fill the position. Were the director and his staff a bunch of bigots? To answer this question I must reflect upon an old saying which goes something like this, "If it smells like a prune and it taste like a prune and it looks like a prune, then it must be a prune."

As my complaint was moving through the system, the job became available again. The director decided to fill the position on a competitive basis. How about that? I wonder where he ever got such a brilliant idea? The man must have been some kind of IRS genius to have come up with the idea I had suggested almost a year earlier and had to file an EEO discrimination complaint to get his attention. His new system of selecting the night manager required all qualified people to be notified of the vacancy and told they could submit a bid for the job.

I didn't put in for the job. The day before the cut off period for applying for the job my division chief, Bob Maddux came storming into my office. He wanted to know why I had not put in for the job. I told him I didn't want the job. His face turned red. He was doing his best not to lose his cool.

He asked, "Why did you file that EEO complaint?"

I replied, "I filed that complaint in order to get you people to open the job up so that all qualified people could compete for the job if they so desired."

He said, "You never did want the job."

I said, "You're right. I never, at any time said I wanted the job. If you guys had considered what EEO is all about and filled the job competitively, you would have never heard from me."

He stormed out of my office faster than he came in. I was less than popular with the director and his staff for a long time. On the other hand, what was new? I had never been popular with the director and his staff.

In the seventeen years I worked for the IRS, the managers never figured out the simplicity of their responsibilities in administering the EEO program. All they were required to do was to ensure that all qualified people had an equal chance to compete for jobs, promotions, training, and special assignments. They were responsible for ensuring the selection process was free of bias. They were required to make a person whole who was not provided the guarantees provided within an EEO program. It is so simple, but those high paid bureaucrats never understood the concept. They continually ended up having to back track and clean up the mess they had created because of their lack of commitment, inadequate insight and an arrogant carelessness in the way they managed the Internal Revenue Services Equal Employment Opportunity program.

A Desire to Serve

In 1978 a memorandum came out of the regional office in San Francisco, soliciting people interested in being an Equal Employment Opportunity (EEO) investigator. This is a part time assignment on an as needed basis. It required a person to leave their regular job for a period of about two weeks to perform an EEO investigation. An investigator performs about two or three investigations a year. I decided this would be a good change of pace. I submitted my name. This was not totally foreign to my background. In the previous office I worked in, I was the Management Analysis Officer. In addition I served as the Equal Employment Opportunity officer.

Of course the IRS rejected my name immediately. Their reason given was that because I was a manager, I could not serve as an EEO investigator. I sent a memo to them and asked where was there a regulation or policy prohibiting a manager from being an investigator? I also said that it made a lot of sense to have a manager as an investigator because a manager understood the ins and outs of the management system. In addition I said the agency should make use of my experience as a former EEO Officer.

I waited for weeks. The deadline for the mandatory training class was drawing near. I called the regional EEO office to talk to my inside source. He said, "Damned, Oscar, you got a hornets nest going. We've been talking to the National Office over your request for days. They can't find any practice or policy to forbid your being an investigator. It looks like you are in." I thanked him and waited. In a few days I received a memorandum appointing me as an investigator and telling me to report to the class.

As an investigator I went to various offices to perform investigations when an employee filed a formal complaint of discrimination. My job was to take testimony of the complainant, the alleged discriminating official (ADO) and any witnesses called by either side. Their testimony was given under oath. I collected all pertinent documentation and provided an analysis of the testimony and data. The completed package was given to the Regional Equal Employment Opportunity Officer for analysis and the development of recommendations to management.

The offices I went to were in racial turmoil. I have never seen so many disgruntled minority employees and so many angry defensive white supervisors. There was a clear-cut pattern. None of the cases involved name calling, white hoods or burning crosses. Almost all of the complaints stemmed from the supervisor giving the employee a low evaluation; or in the view of the employee, the supervisor did not treat them with the same degree of respect as the white employees were accorded; and there were charges that white employees received recognition denied minority employees. This usually revolved around production issues or claims by the ADO's that the employees had attitude problems. As I mentioned earlier, the IRS was big on numbers and small on policy and realistic guide lines. The supervisors were pressed to meet their tax dollar collection quota. They were also being told to meet their quota of minorities. I knew this to be a fact. Like all IRS managers one of the factors in my evaluation was my contribution to the EEO program. The easiest way to meet this criterion was to put some minorities on your staff. The managers in the districts did just what the Regional Office did when they bought me to add a little color to their organization and raise their statistical quota of blacks. The district supervisors bought numbers. They bought people of color.

All people black, white, Hispanic, Asian, and Native American are composed of competent and incompetents.

After the managers bought themselves some minorities to meet their unspoken quota, they stuck them in a corner and forgot about them. A statistical pattern did exist. It showed minorities suffered from more low evaluations than the white employees' population. Was there discrimination? I don't think so. I think the supervisors and minorities were victims of IRS's failed EEO policies. I wanted to yell, "You fools. Can't you see what the numbers game is doing?" But there was no one who would listen. As an investigator I had to present the facts. Statistically the facts were: minority evaluations were generally lower than whites; minorities got fewer promotions; minorities received fewer awards. In essence the facts spoke for themselves.

You may recall when I volunteered to be an EEO investigator, The Regional Office and the National Office said managers couldn't be investigators. They relented when they found there was no regulation or published policy prohibiting a manager from being an investigator. They were smart enough at the time not to suddenly develop such a policy to stop me from becoming an investigator. However, the IRS does not sleep. Two years after I became an investigator, I received a call from the Regional IRS Office informing me that the IRS had developed a policy prohibiting managers from being investigators. I was told I had to turn in my authorization to perform investigations. I didn't get angry or react to this decision. For two years I had been anticipating this action. Just because they rolled over and conceded to my demand to be an investigator didn't mean they were going to play dead. From the time they made the decision to let me become an investigator they had been working on a plan to decertify me.

When I was sticking my authorization into an envelope, I happened to remember old World War Two films where the sergeant had his stripes ripped off of his arm by the commanding officer when he was broken in rank. I drew a picture of sergeant stripes with threads hanging off of them and enclosed the picture with my authorization in an envelope and sent it off to the Regional EEO office. A few days later I got a call from one of the analyst in the Regional EEO Office. He said everyone got a laugh out of my picture.

I am sure that I was the only IRS manager in the whole United States who was an investigator. I did not challenge the taking of my stripes. I figured that in the two years it took the IRS to make their policy, they had checked out all bases with the Treasury Department and their legal eagles, dotted all of their I's and crossed all of their T's. It's very awesome to think they took two years of thinking and plotting to get rid of one manager, who just wanted to serve.

A famous philosopher once said, "Man does not learn from his mistakes, he continues to make the same ones over and over again." The IRS never learns from its mistakes. It continues making the same ones over and over again. About a year after I gave up being an EEO investigator I was called to serve again. A Chinese man came to me and asked me if I would represent him in an EEO discrimination complaint. I listened to his complaint and concluded that it was a strong case. I told him I would be his representative. Under the rules of engagement in the EEO program the option exist for a complainant to select anyone they chose to represent them. When my client sent

my name in as his representative the first response from the
Regional Headquarters was, "No way." They fell back on
the same old jargon of, because I was a manager I could
not represent a complainant. It was deja vu all over again.
My request to serve and the knee jerk reaction of the IRS.
Again I had to refer them to their policies. I had to point
out to them that there was no policy supporting their position. I also informed them that they were denying my client
due process by rejecting me as his representative.

They knew from experience that I was not going to go
away. They didn't agonize too long over my response. They
relented and allowed me to represent my client. In a way
I was surprised. I really didn't think they were that smart!
After my appointment as my clients representative I
explained to him that even though he had a strong case it
would still be a rough road ahead before he saw any kind
of resolution to his complaint. I told him that the IRS will
drag this out as long as they can. It could take as much as
two to three years to get the resolution he wanted. I
explained the process to him which basically is first there
is the informal counseling stage; next follows the investigation stage; often there is a negotiation phase; the next step
is a hearing before an Equal Employment Opportunity
Commission (EEOC) hearing officer; often there is an
appeal. If the complainant wins, the agency will appeal to
the Civil Service Commission. If the agency gets a hearing
ruling in it's favor the complainant may file an appeal; the
Civil Service commission issues a final administrative decision; After that the complainant can go to court.

I could see my client was distressed by the bureaucratic
nonsense he faced. He pepped up a little bit when I told

him I didn't think the IRS would let his case go beyond the investigation because he had a strong case and the IRS hates to lose. I told him that the strength of his case would force them to offer some type of compromise before it went to a hearing. I asked him not to accept a compromise offer from the Region without conferring with me. I didn't want him to fall prey to their intimidation tactics. I knew we could get him something of substance out of this. Before my clients case came to an EEOC hearing the Region contacted him and offered a virtually worthless compromise. He was tired. He couldn't see any progress because of the slow process of the system. The burden was becoming too much to bear. He accepted their offer. I was fit to be tied when he informed me of his agreement to the compromise offer. I wasn't angry at my client. My anger was directed at the people in the Regional Office. It is common courtesy to deal with a client only in the presence of the clients representative. Also, the complainant has the right to demand the presence of his representative. The problem here is the Regional people didn't honor the common courtesy and my client didn't exercise his right. He was bush whacked. I called the Regional EEO representative who was handling my clients case and gave him an earful, but it didn't change the outcome. After my anger had subsided, I had to ask myself whether I was more disappointed at the outcome because I wanted to beat the IRS or was I really concerned about my client? I still don't know the answer to that question. I do believe that the pressure my former client felt from the harassment he was getting from management during the complaint process and the sensitive position he was placed in due to the compromise, led to his stroke and the end of his career a few months after he withdrew his complaint.

Proud as a Peacock

At one of our weekly division staff meetings, our division chief, Glen Coles told us that the Los Angeles District Director was going to be in the center. He said the director had a pet project. It was a movie he had made in his district about the IRS's Western Region which he loved to show to various civic groups. He was proud of his movie and never missed an opportunity to show it to business people at conferences and to IRS personnel when he visited various offices. Our division chief said that he had seen the movie. He wanted us to see the movie. He had invited the district director to show it to us.

We trooped down to one of the training rooms where the movie had been set up. The district director was there. He went into a short speech about how enough isn't done to show the public the good side of the IRS and that is why he took it upon himself to make the movie about the IRS in the Western Region. The movie was only about twenty minutes long. It showed managers planning, secretaries moving about busily and clerks smiling and doing what clerks do. When the movies was over, the director jumped back up to the podium and asked for comments or questions.

There was a long silence. I am sure he expected a lot of accolades. I sat there thinking, what do you do when you invite someone into your house and they insult you? I decided his movie was insulting and I decided to tell him why. I said, "Your movie was very interesting. "The director beamed. I continued, "It shows that all managers in the Western region are white. There was not one minority manager in your movie. Is that what you are trying to portray?" The man was stunned. Before he could speak a female section chief in the Personnel Branch said, "It also shows that all women are regulated to being a secretary or a clerk." The directors face turned beet red. He huffed up and began to defend his movie. He was confused. He tried to convince us that we missed the point. The man had no clue that his movie exposed an ugly hidden agenda of the IRS, which managers like him couldn't begin to see. They had no concept of equal employment opportunity. The media had become sensitive to these issues and would not have produced a film of this type without including minorities and woman in the ranks of managers.

The director continued to sputter his defense. There was subdued snickering from the small audience. Almost everyone was trying to keep from laughing him out of the room. Before he made a bigger fool of himself our division chief moved to the podium by his side. He thanked the director for sharing his movie with us and ushered him out of the room. When our division chief got back he said, "You guys were pretty hard on him." He wasn't visibly upset with us, because he knew us. We were prone to tell it like it was. He wasn't dumb. He knew that we had told the district director the simple truth about his movie. Knowing us like he did, I am surprised that our division chief invited the district director to show us the movie.

Everyone knows a picture is worth a thousand words. It is ironic that a couple of years after the Los Angeles District

Director showed us his movie, the Regional Office made a show and tell movie about the Western Region. Things had changed. There were minority and women managers in this version. There was even what seemed to be a male secretary. I never heard any more about the Los Angeles' Directors film. I wonder if the Regional Office discretely asked him to retire his film?

Fads and Fantasies

I'll say one thing for the IRS, "they believe in keeping up with the Jones'. The IRS is a fad related organization. There are two problems with this. The IRS uses these fads like a child with a new toy. They play act the roles dictated by a particular fad, rather than actually embracing the concept. It's hard to keep up with their characters as they switch fads. The second problem with this fad fetish, is money. It cost money to train people in the latest fad, disband it and move on to the next one. This might be okay for a private enterprise. It's their money they are wasting. However, the IRS is using taxpayers' money to chase the ever fleeting fads.

Team Building/Mind Bending

In 1971 when I went to work for the IRS, everyone seemed to be looking for themselves in drugs or in the many personality altering sensitivity programs which popped up over night. The IRS grabbed this fad and ran with it. It developed a program it called team building. They sent groups of managers to a hotel for a week and in essence tried to brain wash them. There were about twenty people in each group. I got out of being included in the first groups because I told my division chief I had too much work to do in servicing all of the new people coming to the center. I had only hired and trained one employee and she was being worked to death.

We moved into our permanent quarters in 1972. I had hired most of my staff and was in the final stages of training them and settling down into our office routines. I forgot all about the team building group sessions. To my dismay, I found out one more team building group was planned. I thought if I said nothing, I would be forgotten. I wasn't forgotten! My division chief dropped in on me one day. He said, "Oscar, there is one more team building session being planned. The director said that all of those who have not attended will go to this session. I know you are busy but so is everybody else. He is not going to let you off this time."

There wasn't much I could say but, "Okay, Boss."

Our group met in a Salt Lake City hotel for a week. This was costing about $1,200 a day plus round trip transportation cost of about $3000, for a total taxpayers' expense of over $11,000. This does not include the cost of our salaries. Keep in mind that this was just one of a number of sessions.

We broke into small groups and met in hotel rooms which had been set up with a couple of tables. We were encouraged not to contact our offices during our session. We were also encouraged to stay together. In the evening we had a social hour for the total group. The IRS could call this group stuff anything it wanted to but it boiled down to sensitivity training and brain washing. We delved into each other's personality, our strengths, weaknesses, and our lack of commitment to the IRS team. At one time or another, every woman in my six person group cried. I also think I saw a few tears in the men's eyes. We held hands and hugged one another. At times our out pouring of emotions reminded me of a good old, down home church revival. All that was missing was the music, the tambourines and the singing.

Even though we had been in business less than a year, the group had a couple of items for me whereas they believed it demonstrated my lack of commitment to the IRS team. They told me I was aloof. I tried to control the Center by always writing memorandums over the director's signatures. They were right. I admitted they were right. What I didn't admit to them was that I intended to keep right on doing that. They had fun with the aloof thing. They said that I kept everyone at a distance and walked around the Center looking down on everyone. I almost laughed at the "looking down on people" part. After all, I am six feet seven inches tall and it is hard for me to meet the average person eye to eye. I tried to look repentant. I tried not to say what I thought, which was "This is absolute bullshit."

We did have some fun during the week. The one thing I did have in common with a large number of the group was we were heavy drinkers. Here we were in the middle of Mormonville (Salt Lake City). Every night a bunch of us got socked during the social time. Our social time often ended around one in the morning at the swimming pool. One night during an impromptu swim party I was forced to swim in my skives, because I had not brought a swim suit to the pool. By noon the next day someone told me my lack of swim wear had been noted in the Regional Office back in San Francisco. There was also a little hanky panky going on during our stay. It should have been expected with all of us going around hugging; touching;

feeling and getting drunk. I viewed it as part of the team building process. People who sleep together get very close. Finally the sensitivity fad dissipated and the IRS was off in search of the next fad.

Off Site–Out of Sight

Another fad the IRS got into was the offsite seminar or conference thing. The IRS paid for hundreds of expensive conference rooms and training rooms for the service centers, regional and district offices. Did we use them? No! We had to go to resorts like Asilomar near Santa Cruz, California or local hotels to discuss our business because the expensive conference rooms and training rooms were too close to the work we were supposed to be discussing and directing. Management felt we needed the seclusion so that we could talk about the work we had left behind.

The Western Region's Regional Commissioner, his staff, and support group made it a point to go to Asilomar. Asilomar is a lovely secluded place on the Pacific Ocean. From Asilomar you can the famous Pebble Beach golf course and the beautiful Carmel Bay. It's a stones throw from Monterey California. One of my close acquaintances who attended this offsite seance said, the only thing he got out of it was to sleep with his boss. She was female. The funny part of this was, he said, "she was so drunk she didn't even remember it the next day."

In Fresno, California we were cheapies. We rented a few local hotel rooms for the day. Before the off site fad started we held our annual production meetings and division managers' meetings in our conference or training rooms.

No one bothered us because we put our assistants in charge and told them not to interrupt us until the meetings were over. In the off site hotel rooms we sat around talking about the same things we would have talked about if we had met at the Center. These offsite seances were informal. We brought our own booze. One time we had a no hoist bar. At work most of the managers wore suits, ties, etc. At the off-sites, we wore jeans, boots, and sport shirts. I never did figure out the significance of this. How did this enhance management effectiveness? How did it enhance communication? What was the point? I forgot to mention that the Asilomar resort and hotel accommodations, as well as subsistence and travel expenses for overnight stays, were paid for by you, the taxpayer. The offsite stuff finally fizzled out and we ended up eventually using our high-priced conference and training rooms to hold our seances.

Build a Better Box

In the late eighties quality teams were the fad? I think it started with the automobile manufactures. On television automobile manufactures touted their quality teams, usually consisting of a designer, an engineer, a foreman and a couple of workers. The IRS bought this fad hook, line, and sinker.

Quality teams started popping up in all of the districts, the service centers and the regional offices. You were nobody if you were not on a quality team. Almost every manager I knew was on a team. The quality teams were given assignments to resolve some form of a problem or to improve some facet of a system.

I was assigned to a regional office quality team. My team consisted of the Fiscal Officer from the San Jose District; our Regional Chief of the Accounting Section; the Accounting Unit Chief; our Regional travel expert; and myself. Our team was assigned the job of coming up with an improved system for processing obligating documents, vendor payments, moving expense and travel vouchers at the service centers, districts and in the Regional office. We met once a week in the regional office. This meant that each week, for months I had to go up to San Francisco from Fresno. Usually I flew my plane. If the weather was too bad to fly my plane, I took a commercial airline or rented a car. It really didn't make any difference how I got there, the IRS was paying for it. We usually started our meetings at ten o'clock. I wasn't the dedicated type of person who would spend his time traveling home in the evening on my time. I usually stayed overnight in San Francisco and returned to Fresno the following morning.

The quality teams were given no specific time to complete their projects. The only mandate was that they meet once each week. The purpose of this mandate was to insure that teams did not just die on the vine by postponing their meetings indefinitely. Our team was finally buried by the quantity of documents, statistics and procedures we had collected.

We worked hard in trying to come to some form of closure. With such a varied group of people, it was difficult to move in one direction. Part of our problem was the wide latitude of our assignment. There were a multitude of things which could be improved. It seemed to me I might spend the rest of my career commuting to San

Francisco working with the team. Normally I looked forward to going to San Francisco, but I was getting a little tired of making the trek to the region every week. After a few months of commuting I suggested to our team leader that she let me take all of our data back to Fresno and let me try to draft a final report for the team. She agreed.

I spent a few days preparing the report. I am an opinionated person. I had always had opinions as to how the system could be improved. I simply incorporated the statistics and other data we had collected into a proposal which supported my opinions. Voila, we had a final report. I had my secretary type a draft and I sent it to our team leader. She liked it. She presented it at the next meeting. They rest of the team were just as tired of meeting as I was. At that point I don't think the team cared what was in the final report, as long as we had one.

We put the report in its final form. The team leader set up a meeting with the Assistant Regional Commissioner for Human Resources. We gave him the big dog and pony show (show and tell). He played the part and acted as if he was impressed. He congratulated us on our achievements. The team was disbanded. I don't remember any of our proposals ever being implemented. In fact I can say with certainty that not one suggested improvement made by the team was ever implemented. I believe that was the result of most, if not all of the quality teams' reports. The reports sat in the file and like the teams they faded away. A funny thing about the IRS and fades is that there is no formal declaration that the fad is ended. There was no official word that the quality team fad was over. One by one the teams died. Then there were no more.

Weights and Measures

The IRS is not unlike other organizations in its need to evaluate employees. The majority of employees are on production so it is a fairly easy task to establish an evaluation system based upon production and error rate. When it came to supervisors and managers the IRS had for many years used the old standard forms whereas the evaluator checked a series of items from excellent down to poor . Usually a small bit of nebulous narrative was included to add some kind of validity.

You know the IRS. Somebody read a new book on management and found that some industries were starting to evaluate its executives on goals set at the beginning of the rating period. Over night, before the sun could rise we had a new evaluation systems for managers. Under the new system each manager had to set goals for his organization to accomplish. These goals had to be coordinated with the next highest level of management and with the managers regional counterparts. Think of the problems most IRS managers had in setting goals for their organization. Most private businesses exist to make a profit. Their managers can set an increased profit goal. However, the IRS is not a business which makes a profit. None of the IRS managers could use an increase in profit as a goal. Private industry also had a number of other items it could set as goals for its managers. They could and did use production; sales; new clients; and a number of other meaningful factors related to an industry. We IRS managers couldn't use these goals because we had no control over production; clients; and we certainly didn't sell anything.

So there I sat, like many IRS managers scratching my head and mumbling how stupid this new evaluation system was. I realized I had to play the game. I set about making some objectives. I had two things in my favor. The first was my division chief wasn't that familiar enough with the internal operations of my office. This wasn't a knock on him there was no reason for him to get that involved. This meant I could probably make up any kind of objectives I wanted to. Some of the Regional people I had to coordinate the goals with could be a problem if they really got involved. I don't know about other IRS managers but I saw a threat in this new evaluation system. What if you set a bunch of goals and failed to meet them? Could that be a ticket out the door if someone had it in for you?

My mother didn't raise a dummy. I set about making goals which I knew we could accomplish or had accomplished before. For example, I got a weekly error report from the head of my Timekeeping/Payroll function. I looked back through the previous years history of the error reports and set error rate goals which I knew we couldn't miss beating. Up to this point only my Timekeeping/Payroll supervisor and I knew about this report because it was an internal thing I had set up for my information. I set up a separate system for keeping records for achieving my goal. I used the same technique for setting my budget formulation and execution goals; vendor invoice processing goals; voucher processing goals; and goals for the management analysis function. That was an easy one. What kind of measurable goals can you set for a management analyst? I made the goal for the analyst the number of studies I wanted accomplished a year. Who set the number of studies? Me!

I think you the reader is getting a feel for how foolish the system was. At the end of the year I wrote a report on how I met my goals. My division chief looked at them and nodded his, "Okay." When the regional people came down to the center for their evaluation, we quibbled a little over some of the numbers, but they nodded their heads, "Okay." Now another problem arose. Unless something significant within your organization has changed how can you keep setting higher goals for the same functions. I kept waiting for the fad to die. In the third year of this program I was getting desperate for goals. I got an idea. I dug out my goals of two years ago and recycled them. My secretary knew what I was doing and she was getting a good laugh as she was retyping the goals from two years ago into next year. No one noticed. My division chief and the regional folks just nodded their heads. This fad finally burned itself out. It had to because the system had to start rolling back upon itself as it did with me as I began to recycle my goals. We sort of migrated back into the old system of check marks and nebulous narratives.

Before Their Time

When the personal computers hit the market, the IRS started buying these clunks by the bushels. They didn't waste time identifying what use we might make of them. I call them clunkers because the first ones they bought were a bunch of the old eight inch floppy disk types. I believe they were Hewlett Packard. It has been so long that I don't remember the model. Everyone was trying to get into the classes to learn how to run those relics.

I didn't go to the class nor did I sign up any of my employees to go. Everyone thought I was anti-computer. That was not the case. I was anti-junk. I had a background in electronics. I was in electronics in the service; my major in college was electronics; and I once owned a radio and television repair store. I believe I could have built one of those old relics. Because of my electronic background and having kept up with the industry I felt it would be a waste of my time and my staff's time playing with what I considered to be a Model A Ford. I knew the following generations of machines would be more practical and usable. Another factor in my thinking was the fact my office had a programable calculator. My programable calculator could out perform the dinosaur computers which first entered the market. Before I could say," junk pile," all of those old relics had been stored in a training room where they sat for a long time gathering dust. Their next move was to the trash bin. The IRS did not use one of these machines to accomplish any task relating to work.

When the IRS began to move into the modern era computer, I was quick to get an IBM-XT. Soon after that I acquired an IBM-AT for my immediate staffs use. A few years later I got a Texas Instruments machine just for the purpose of updating two expert systems I had developed for my office. This is a story within itself which I will share with you in another chapter. I also got a couple of XTs for my timekeeping staff.

The most comical thing about the whole process was obtaining the new machines. Along with the requisition, there had to be a written justification which included a projection of staff year savings. The total of all of my projected staff year savings to justify the purchase of my computers, exceeded the number of people I had on my immediate staff. By purchasing some computers I had saved my staff right out of existence. Yet each day I arrived at work there they were. The simple truth is that my people could have continued to do their job without ever having one computer in the office. The IRS had to rationalize some way of justifying the purchase of computers. They arbitrarily picked projected staff years savings. Many years after the advent of the computer many companies realized that computers don't necessarily reduce the number of employees. The personal computer simply made it easier for the employees to do some of their jobs. When I left the organization the IRS was still operating under the false assumption that personal computers had saved a significant amount of manpower.

Their savings were made up from offices like mine whose requisition records showed I had saved my office out of existence. This was not a unique experience. Throughout the IRS this facade of saving staff years through the purchase of personal computers was being practiced in every office. Yet the IRS could not point to one instance whereas the purchases resulted in the reduction of one person or a reduction in hiring goals. Another phenomenon which occurred as a result of the computer acquisitions was the thief of software. A number of managers and analyst copied the software which was purchased by the IRS to be used on IRS computers. Some of them attempted to rationalize the thefts by saying they used their personal computers at home to do IRS work. If you, the reader believe that, then please consider purchasing the bridge I have in my back yard for sale.

An Expert–A Former Drink of Water

In the late eighties, the flash words were, expert systems. Computer companies were pushing them on television. I had read some excellent articles on expert systems. I was intrigued by the concept. It just so happens I had a buddy in the Center who was up to his eyeballs in computers. He was a genuine nerd. He was also a very nice person. His name is Rudy. Rudy was in a strange situation. He belonged to the Research Computer Section in the National Office in Washington, D.C. Because of personal reasons, he was allowed to be located in the Fresno Service Center.

He was put under the administrative control of our computer branch in the Data Conversion and Accounting Division. They didn't know how or didn't care to make use of his services. He sat off in a little corner by himself, surrounded by his computers and peripheral support equipment. He was an outcast. For some reason, I am always drawn to these kind of people. Maybe it's the instinct to watch out for the under dog. Rudy had helped me and my staff develop some elaborate coupled electronic worksheets for our budget projections and tracking systems. My staff adopted Rudy.

It should have been no surprise what he said when I asked him what he knew about expert systems. He was well versed on the subject. He had taught himself how to develop them and had obtained a Texas Instrument computer especially designed to develop and update expert systems. Likewise it should have been no surprise to find out that the National Office computer research folks were already chasing this fad and were trying to develop some expert systems.

He showed me a flow process chart showing how an expert system functioned. It was very similar to what I called a critical path chart. I used them when I was in industrial engineering in the Sixties. Some people called them decision making charts. When I was in contract administration on the Atlas Missile Program, we required General Dynamics to use these charts in tracking their progress on the work at the Atlas missile sites. A critical path chart simply starts at one point, moves to a junction where there are two or more alternatives. After selecting an alternative, the process continues until you arrive at an answer to your problem or the completion of a project. This is the same process which an expert system uses to lead the user to a solution to his problem.

My friend said, except for me no one in his division knew or cared that he could develop an expert system. In fact no one in the service center had even talked to him about one. He told me the National Office had been trying to develop an expert system but to date they had not been successful. I asked him how he would like to be the first one in the IRS to develop a functional operating expert system. He began to drool.

Rudy had the technical know-how to make an expert system. He needed someone who was an expert in some field to give him the data to design the system around and work with him during the design. I had plenty of time to devote to the project since I had recently down sized my operation from twenty-six people to five by getting rid of the timekeeping/payroll, management analysis, and quality assurance functions. The remaining five people were so proficient in their jobs, they didn't need me looking over their shoulders. For four or five weeks, I spent the majority of my time working with Rudy on the development of two expert systems.

I selected two simple systems which I thought we could handle. I didn't think it was wise to take on a huge grandiose project like a budget projection or budget execution. I wanted something without too many variables which we could get mired down in. I think that was the mistake the National Office was making. One of the systems I chose was payroll problem solving. The other was travel voucher preparation. My partner worked on this project day, night and weekends. A couple of times he came over to my house on a weekend to review some of the critical path changes or user help insertions to be sure they were in the right places. The help items were the biggest challenge. They are inserted at key junctions so that if a person was not sure which choice to make he could ask for help and be told what options each junction provided. The problem with them was they had to be specific, not too long but yet they had to be clear enough so that a laymen, could understand which choice to make.

We finally had the two systems ready. We set up a show and tell for the director and his staff. My buddy ran the program as I walked them through the two systems. The programs were displayed on a large reverse screen projection. Everyone seemed to be very interested in the programs, except for the Chief of the Data Conversion and Accounting Division, where my buddy was assigned. Everyone else was asking questions and genuinely seemed impressed, except

Rudy' division chief. He sat there. Stone faced. He tried his best to look as bored as he could. You would think since it was his employee getting these accolades that he would at least show some type of recognition. Small people have a large problem in trying to hide jealousy. Hiding behind his protracted boredom just made Rudy's division chief look that much sillier. I know he didn't have the most basic understanding of the functions of an expert system. I must take some blame for Rudy' division chief's attitude. In our haste to set up the show and tell I had forgotten to ask Rudy to brief his division chief ahead of time. I can say his division chief lived up to my expectations. I had always thought he was a little person, with little substance and his little act seemed to validate my opinion.

When the national office heard about our two functioning systems, three of their people jumped on a plane to Fresno. We demonstrated the systems for them. They were very enthusiastic about what we had done and asked to take copies of our systems back with them. We were more than happy to oblige them.

This expert system thing was another case whereas the IRS was trying to keep up with a fad. I jumped into the fad because I was bored and had a lot of time on my hands after completing my office down sizing. On the other hand the National Office people were wrestling with bears, in trying to develop some complicated and grandiose expert systems to help in the tax collection system. They were in way over their heads. There were contractors which had become specialists in the field of developing expert systems. The smart thing for the IRS's national office people to do would have been to first objectively assess whether there was a real need for an expert system. If there was a true need, which I don't believe there was, they should have contracted with an established vendor to develop their systems. They National Office people were looking for Pandora's box. This fad like all of the others faded away. If you mentioned expert systems to IRS employees, today you would only get a blank stare.

Shortly after we finished our project, Rudy transferred back to the national office. I was sorry to see him go because I had been reading up on the latest computer fad, "Neural networks." If he had stayed in Fresno, maybe we could have developed the first functioning IRS neural network.

A neural network mimics the function of the human brain; it makes rational decisions; it can learn; doesn't make the same mistakes repeatedly; has no jealousy; and doesn't get big fat bonuses for doing its job. We could have developed a system which could have been used to replace all of the highly paid managers in the IRS. Wouldn't that be a healthy change from the old trial by error management style?

See All–Hear Too Much

Remember the open landscape fad? Of course the IRS had to be a part of this. In the seventies most of the new offices went to the open landscape layout. At the Fresno Service Center the administration building housed the Human Resource Division, the director and assistant director's offices and all of the division and assistant division chiefs. This meant that when a person walked into the building, he saw a sea of partitions, tall ones for important people and short ones for not so important people. I had tall ones. There were no clear cut aisles, so a person needing personnel, fiscal or facilities assistance had to meander among the partitions, looking over or around each one until he found the person he wanted.

Maybe open landscape would suit something like a boiler room operation where people are basically tied to their desk and there is no reason for a lot of traffic. With six thousand people to service, you can imagine the traffic in the Administration Building. The partitions were always being knocked askew by people meandering among them. People had a habit of leaning on the shorter ones and talking to someone rather than going around and entering through the opening. The Facilities Management Branch probably spent three staff years each year trying to keep the partitions straight. I think after a few years, they just gave up. Sometimes I would stand and look around, and the skewed partitions reminded me of a bunch of drunk sailors walking into a high wind.

In order to make the open landscape look less like a desert isle, the IRS spent hundreds of thousands of dollars to by plants and stick them among the partitions. In Fresno we spent thirty thousand dollars on plants. There was no rationale for the placement of these plants. They were just more obstacles for people to bump into. In addition to the purchase cost of the plants each office spent at least five thousand dollars a year for a maintenance contract to take care of these plants.

No one I knew liked the open landscape. There was no privacy. If I or any other manager wanted to council, an employee, we had to schedule one of four little conference rooms. I also had situations whereas a worker might become belligerent with my staff concerning a payroll problem. I had to take the person into my office to try and calm him down. With the open landscaping, everyone within one hundred feet of me could still hear what was going on.

One bright day I walked by the director's office. All of the partitions around the director and the assistant director's offices were gone. Framing for private offices were being put up. I asked the director's secretary what was going on. She said that one day, some union members were seen eavesdropping outside of the director's partition. The director decided that he and the assistant director needed more privacy. I wonder if this guy ever stopped to think that anything that was discussed in his office had been discussed at a number of lower management levels where everyone had open landscape? Why is it that when the problem got to the directors office it suddenly became an issue to discuss in private behind closed doors? The IRS should have bitten the bullet and put in private offices for those who would normally have a private office when they put in the director's office. It was not to be. When I left the place, those partitions were still leaning into the wind and the plants were being shoved here and there.

Talking about the IRS being caught up in the open land scape fad reminded me of the perverse thinking process the IRS uses to justify it's end in planning where to place it's various offices. The Fresno Service was constructed in Fresno, California because the president had issued an executive order stipulating that all federal offices were to be constructed in cities which have a high unemployment. At the time Fresno had a very high unemployment rate. In fact it still does. When the decision was made to place the service center in Fresno a hot debate centered around the question of which part of town should it be in? The logic dictated that it should be closest to the area with the people who suffer the highest unemployment. In Fresno, that would be the West side.

Like many cities the black ghetto and a portion of the barrio are located on the West side of Fresno, on the other side of the tracks.

The debate went like this. It was agreed that there was a large group of unemployed people on the west side of town. It was populated primarily by blacks with a smattering of Hispanics. It amounted to probably no more than thirteen percent of the city's population. On the other hand the bulk of the seasonal work force would certainly be white. It was suggested that many whites would not work in the center if it was placed in West Fresno because of fear for their safety. After much debate and agonizing the service center, which eventually would have a work force of over six thousand was placed in the far Southeast corner of Fresno. This was right on the outskirts of the most expensive areas in Fresno called Sunny Side. The IRS could have paid a third of the cost for their lease if they had built the service center on the westside of town.

Just recently, in 1998 the San Jose District's office in Fresno was moved from downtown, in the low rent area to the North part of town in the high rent area. The building downtown had ample parking for employees and taxpayers and it was in a low traffic volume. The owner of the building offered to make any renovations the IRS wanted to keep them downtown. The mayor, the city council, the downtown business owners and the chamber of Commerce tried to get the IRS to leave the office down town. The General Services Administration who let the contract for the building in the high rent area said, "we didn't make the decision. The IRS made the decision to move."

The IRS kept throwing out a number of nebulous reasons for making the move and finally in it's last statement of defense it said, "We are moving so that we can be nearer the people we serve." They moved their office to the Northern portion of the city which is an area populated by the well off, with beautiful and expensive business complexes. Why would the IRS have to situate it's self near a certain group of people, whom it claims to serve? It has been my experience that the people where-ever they may be, found their way to the IRS office to which they were summoned.

Well, here we are in Fresno with two IRS offices. They just happen to be in the two most expensive areas in the city. The district office which moved to the high rent district is now paying almost two third more for it's lease. It is also located in a high volume traffic area. Now there is one more perfectly good building left empty downtown.Toward the end of my tenure with the IRS there was a lot of talk about down sizing the regional offices. There was talk about moving the Accounting section to one of the Service Centers. There seemed to be a feeling that it would be sent to Fresno and become part of my office. There was talk of sending the analyst who supported the districts out to the district offices. In the midst of all of this talk there evolved a plan to move the regional office to the Walnut creek area, about forty miles East of San Francisco. This last bit of talk got my attention more than any of the rest because I couldn't see why the regional office would be moved out to the suburbs, from San Francisco. When I heard about this part of the plan I asked a number of people why? Finally one of the regional managers asked me a question. He asked, "Who lives out in the area they want to move the headquarters to?" I told him I had no idea. He said, "the regional commissioner, and almost all of his staff live out there." Some of the rational given for this proposal was it would save money because the leasing cost of property in the suburbs would be cheaper than San Francisco. How devious the IRS manager's minds work. In Fresno they were not looking for cheap. In fact they were not looking for cheap in Walnut Creek. They were looking at getting rid of their long commute in the morning and evening. They were thinking of the big, "Me, me, me!"

After I retired much of the planning became reality as the regional offices downsized. However, because of the political impact the regional office in the Western Region was left in San Francisco.

Candy in a Baby's Hand

Another fad the IRS fell right into was that of issuing credit cards to frequent travelers. My office had the responsibility of managing the program. I thought it was a bad idea to begin with but I didn't have a choice. The only real benefit I could see from the program was the credit card company which sold the IRS on this idea would make more money. The theory behind the program was that by not giving cash advances to our travelers, more cash would be in the treasury and hence the government would pay less interest for money to run the government. Can't you just hear some high paid credit card lobbyist pumping this story up some IRS executive's rear end over an expense paid lunch?

When I authorized the issuance of a credit card to one of our frequent travelers, he was told to not use this card for personal purchases. Primarily the people receiving the cards were managers and supervisors. A few specialists who traveled often were given cards. Within a few months, personal purchases were beginning to show up on the monthly listing which I got from the credit card company. The listing showed all purchases a person had made, i.e., the date, the company, the merchandise, and the cost. It had another section for delinquent accounts.

I had not told anyone that my office would be getting this monthly listing. I didn't purposely hide the information. I just didn't see a need to publicize it. As the number of personal purchases began to climb, I felt obligated to send out a memorandum reminding people they were not supposed to use the government issued credit cards for personal use. I told them about the listing I received each month from the credit card company. There was a stream of people coming or calling my office to assure me that they would pay off their personal debt and not make anymore. One of those people was the Assistant Division Chief of the Data Conversion and Accounting Division.

Our outstanding accounts of over three months old began to grow. In theory there should be not outstanding accounts, because when employees finished a trip, they turned in a travel voucher. They were reimbursed for the trip and were expected to use the money to clear their credit card. Many employees were receiving their travel reimbursement and spending it, leaving their credit card account unpaid. This was beginning to upset the credit card company because as part of their sales pitch to the IRS they had agreed not to charge our employees any interest on the outstanding balance. They assumed that employees would liquidate their outstanding balance soon after their trip was completed. The credit card company had planned to make their profit from the business related travel our employees made. They never anticipated lending interest free money VIA their credit card. Even though employees had been warned not to use the cards for personal use, the incidences of personal charges to credit cards began to escalate. Overdue accounts continued grow.

I took the position that it wasn't my problem. I felt that my job was to see that the employees turned in their vouchers and were reimbursed for their travel. As far as I was concerned, collecting the outstanding balances on the credit card was the credit card company's problem. However, about a year after the credit cards were issued, I got a call from the Regional Fiscal Officer. He expressed his concern about the number of delinquent credit card accounts we had at the service center. I conveyed my sympathies to him and added my opinion that this was not an IRS problem. It was the credit card company's problem. I pointed out to him that we had insured that the employees turned in their vouchers and were reimbursed. I felt my responsibility ended there. He didn't agree with my position. He put out a memorandum to all employees in the Western Region informing them not to use their government issued travel credit card for personal purchases. In his memorandum he also reminded them to promptly turn in their travel vouchers after completing their travel. Because of the use of the credit cards, late submission of travel vouchers had become a problem. Some employees weren't concerned about getting reimbursed quickly because expenses had been charged to their credit card.

When I retired in 1988, the credit card problem was still plaguing the IRS. After I had been retired for over two years, I got a call at my home from a branch chief. She was upset because her division chief was threatening to give her a suspension of three days without pay for using her IRS credit card for personal purchases. She wanted to know what the policy was when I was the fiscal officer. I don't see how she could have forgotten. She was there when I issued my memorandum saying the card should not be used for personal purchases. I reminded her it was the same then as it apparently is now—no personal purchases. I reminded her that I had put out a memorandum stating that. I don't think that helped her much. I believe that eventually the three-day suspension she faced was reduced to one day.

Considering the problems, the general population has with credit cards, i.e. maxing them out, not liquidating the amount due, why would the IRS think its employees would be any different? If you put candy in a child's hands, he is going to eat it. If you put an interest free credit card into the hands of many people, they are going to use it and abuse it!

Awards

Monetary performance awards are supposed to be given to those who achieve some type of performance far in excess of what is expected of them. In the agencies I worked in for twenty years prior to going to work for the IRS, monetary performance awards were a rare exception, not the rule. If someone got a monetary performance award, the exceptional accomplishment of the individual could easily be discerned from that of what was expected of him or her. I had received two monetary performance awards in the twenty years of my career prior to going to work for the IRS. That was a very good record. Most people never received a monetary performance award in their whole career. In addition to the monetary awards I received bushel baskets of letters of commendation and appreciation.

The system of awards within the IRS is nothing more than a system which awards people for doing their job. Hundreds of thousands of taxpayers' dollars are being paid to high and mid level cronies for doing their job. I kept a file that I called, "The Fat Cats File." Some of the awards were down right obscene. In this chapter I share with the reader some of the most bizarre reasons the IRS rationalized for giving monetary awards.

The Most Ludicrous Award

In the mid eighties we were bursting at our seams. We needed more space. The decision was made to lease some off-site warehouse space to store our hundreds of thousands of files. An up and comer, a section chief in the Facilities management Branch named Eddie, was given the job of getting the off-site warehouse ready. This type of work is a normal job for a facilities management organization.

I had coined a nickname for the section chief in charge of this project. I called him, Fast Eddie. The reason for this is that every time I saw him walking down the aisle, he was moving like a power walker; at top speed; hair back; and nose into the wind. He talked as fast as he walked. I have always been dubious of anyone with such a fast lip. I have my doubts that their brain can keep up with their mouth. I commented to my supervisor of my timekeeping/payroll function, who had this same tendency, that if a person is always in a hurry, he must always be late. Of course she didn't agree with this observation. That's why later on, as part of her training I used to go by her office in the morning and invite her to walk around the center with me. I made her walk at my pace, a slow leisurely pace. To this day she has not forgiven me for this.

Near the end of Eddie's project, it was time to move the files to the new warehouse. Fast Eddie and his employees were in a hurry. They removed the bracing which tied the tops of the old shelving together. These shelves were about eight feet tall and stood in long rows. They probably covered an area of twenty yards by fifty yards. They removed the bracing before they removed the files. The shelves started falling over. Like dominoes, one fell on the other and bump, bump, bump...they all fell down. Thousands of files which had once been in boxes were now strewn all over the floor.

The division chief of the division responsible for the files was incensed. she wrote a memorandum to me complaining that in their haste to move the files to the new warehouse, our Facilities Management Branch employees had cost her twenty-five hundred staff hours, at a cost of $10,000 to get the files back in order. The estimated cost reflected the staff hour wages used to rectify the problem. I think she underestimated the true cost because she didn't cost in any of the personnel benefits which would make the loss more like $13,000. However, $10,000 is still a lot of money to throw away because someone was in a hurry. She wanted to be reimbursed for the loss. I wrote her a memorandum increasing her divisional allowance of staff hours to reimburse her for the loss.

After the new warehouse was set up and operating, my division chief, good old Glenn, came hopping into my office. He asked, "Is there any more money left in my awards fund?"

I asked, "How much do you need?"

He said, "About two or three hundred. The director thinks Eddie (Fast Eddie) should get an award for bringing the off-site warehouse in ahead of schedule."

I was stunned. I was speechless for a moment, which is a rarity for me. When my speech returned, I said, "If you deduct the amount of the $13,000 his people cost us from the award you are going to give him, he still owes us over $12,000."

Glen got a little defensive. He said, "The director thinks he deserves an award and I am going to give him one." He turned and stormed out of my office. Glen didn't need my approval to give awards. He asked me about the availability of funds because I was the Financial Officer. I knew that, but I couldn't help telling him about the real world whereas he was going to give an award for a complete screw up.

I wasn't there when the director made his comment about giving an award to Fast Eddie. But consider the facts. Fast Eddie was the man who made the schedule which he beat. The director, Theron Polivka had no way knowing if the schedule was a realistic one or not? What did he know about warehouses? Nothing of course. He probably made a passing comment about, Fast Eddie, doing a good job. Like most, yes men, my division chief was off and running. If my chief had any balls and was doing his job, he would have reminded the director about the $13,000 screw up. On second thought, the director would still have given fast Eddie an award. After all, there is no way the incensed division chief, whose people had to clean up the files mess, didn't inform the director of her displeasure with Fast Eddie's crew.

The Most Outrageous Award

If the preceding was the most ludicrous example I had seen of the IRS's award program, then what I am going to describe must be the most outrageous example. In the late eighties, the chief of Personnel Branch gave each and every one of his employees in the branch a performance award, except for his secretary. It was alleged that he didn't give his secretary an award because they didn't get along. His branch had about forty people.

This was pushing the envelope, even for the IRS. It caused all kinds of morale problems. Most of the other employees in the Human Resources Division were asking, "why not me?" My employees were a good example of that. In my staff meetings, my immediate staff kept bringing it up. "Why not us? We work just as hard as those people in Personnel." I tried to explain to them that awards were not meant to be given to people for just doing the job they were being paid to do.

They still came back with, why them and not us? They reminded me that I had only given out one award in fifteen years. That was in 1972. She was the first employee I hired. I gave her a performance award because I strongly believed she went far beyond what was expected of her. She had to run our new office for a week during the early part of our tenure because I had to go to a stupid sensitivity training class. She had hardly any training at the time, but she carried on without me. In many other aspects she exceeded my expectations.

I got tired of hearing my employees complaints about not getting any awards. I asked myself, "Why are you trying to protect the integrity of the system which has no integrity?" I decided to start writing some awards–why not? It's the IRS way to give people performance awards for doing their job. I had not heard any complaints from my timekeeping function but I thought I should include them also. I instructed the supervisor of the timekeeping function to give a group award to all of the timekeepers. Each one was giventwenty-five dollars and a certificate telling them what good employees they were. That took care of seventeen people. I wrote the justification for an individual award for my timekeeping supervisor and the rest of my immediate staff. When I sent my awards forward for the approval of my division chief, Bob Maddux, he called me in to talk. He said, "If I approve these awards, that would give everyone in your organization an award." I repeated what my people had been harping to me. I asked, "Why Personnel employees and not mine?"

He said, "I'm taking a lot of heat over that."

I said, "I am, too. My employees are ready to mutiny."

He thought a while and said, "What do you think of my approving half now and half some time later?"

We struck a deal. My timekeepers had already been given their awards. That left just my immediate staff. We agreed to give half of my staff awards immediately and half later. I decided to give the lower graded employees their awards first. Three months later, I gave the remaining awards. I had become a real IRS manager. I had given out twenty-five awards to people for simply coming to work and doing their job. I had arrived!

The Most Obscene Award

The most obscene monetary award I saw given in the IRS was given to me. In the late eighties, we were in our weekly Human Resources Division staff meeting (Show and tell). Our division chief had a printout of the awards given by division, grade, and race. He said our division was noticeably short on awards for minority managers. He said we had to take a look at that area. After the meeting my buddy and I went to have a coffee. Over coffee I said to him, "In a few months, at the end of the next rating period, one of us is going to get a performance award."

He asked, "What are you talking about?"

I said, "There are only three minority managers who could get awards and raise our division statistics. One is you (a Hispanic), two is me (a black), and there is our new training branch chief (a Hispanic). The new branch chief is a personal friend of our chief, but he is too new in the organization, so that just leaves you and me." When you play a numbers game with race and a limited number of people, it is fairly easy to predict the outcome.

A few months later, I got a $1500 performance award. If any thing my performance in the last couple of years had gone down because I had reduced my staff by over twenty people and I was just laying back coasting into retirement. I got the performance award because I am black. That is obscene. I didn't run around the Center shouting, "Look at me! I got a performance award." I didn't take much pride in being given an award because of my race. I didn't earn it. I did nothing to qualify for the award other than to stand in the sun enough to insure my tan was showing. Since I felt no pride in receiving the award one might wonder why I didn't give it back. The answer is very simple. My mother didn't raise a fool!

As soon as I was told about the award I looked up my buddy and reminded him of our discussion a few months earlier. He said, "You sure called that one." Each year I continued to get a performance award. It was scaled down to $1000 a year because the director and his staff set up a tier system for monetary awards whereas division chiefs were given a certain amount, branch chiefs received less, section chiefs less, etc. You see my initial $1500 put me at the division chief award level. We couldn't have that could we? On the other hand consider why the director would establish a pecking order for awards. If a reward is given based upon performance, it should be commensurate to the performance. Isn't it possible a branch chief has out performed a division chief?

In May of 1988 when I filed my papers to retire, my division chief said, "You know if you stay until the end of the rating period, (September 30) you will get an award."

I said, "Thank you but I'm getting out of here while I still have my sanity." Don't be too critical of my division chief. One shouldn't hold his proposal against him. He was just doing it the IRS way.

The Invisible Accomplishments

Another thing I could never understand about the IRS awards system is the technique of assigning someone to a task force or other special assignment and rewarding them for completing the job. I have tried to rationalize this. When I assigned someone to a special project or a task force I did it because I thought they had the experience, the expertise and could accomplish the assignment. In other words it was just another job assignment. IRS manager's expectations must be different from mine. They apparently are surprised the people they assign to task forces or other special assignments complete the task they were assigned. The IRS manager feels he must award the people because they completed the assigned task. Isn't that a strange paradox?

It's not like these people are not being paid their regular salary, because they are. When people are assigned to special assignments often, they are relieved of their usual duties. In essence they are assigned to another full time job. Where is the difficulty? When our director was placed on a task force for a number of months the assistant director ran the center. Isn't that why we have assistants, to fill in the absence of the big cheese? When the director's task force had completed the assignment he got a $10,000 performance award. I call giving awards for doing what is expected, "The invisible accomplishment." If you look very closely at what these task forces accomplish, you cannot identify the superior accomplishments for which the members are being awarded. If the people on them are competent, they accomplish what they were told to do. Big deal. This does not constitute work above and beyond the call of duty. Sometimes they don't accomplish any thing, but they always get a monetary award.

A good example of the process of giving monetary performance awards to task force members, for invisible accomplishments, was a task force was set up to do the planning for redistricting the region. When the task force had completed their job in 1983, all of them got awards for doing the job. There was a pecking order to the awards. This is the old IRS system whereas the higher graded employees on the task force get more than the lower graded ones.

Some of the awards given were:

Task Force Chairwoman	$5000
Member, Fresno Service Center Division Chief	$2000
Member, Regional Management Analyst	$1000

There were smaller awards for each lower graded task force member. Everyone secretary, clerk and gopher on the task force got a monetary award. I don't think you can find anyone who has been assigned to a task force or a special assignment in the IRS who was not given an award when the job had completed. The question which keeps cycling through my mind is, "Why do you award a person whom you place on a task force for doing the job they were put there to do?" I still don't understand why and for sure, the IRS is not telling.

Fun Things

I have titled this chapter, "Fun Things." The reason for this is I had so much fun in participating in these events. To some degree they were adversarial or competitive. I like a good fight. I like competition. Because of the large egos and limited insight of the IRS managers with whom I was dealing with, I felt I had a distinct advantage in the exchanges. For some reason I often appeared to be at odds with the IRS management system. I was a member of the system, but I usually was marching to a different beat. I can say with some pride I never lost a battle or the war when we went head to head.

My Greatest Coup

I think my greatest coup in the seventeen years I spent with the IRS was my getting them to give me a three-month expense-paid vacation. I was offered four months but one can only take so much of a good thing. My greatest coup began one day in 1984. Bob Maddux, my division chief came into my office. He sat down and threw his feet up on my desk. I knew that I was in for some heavy bull-shit. This was my second of three division chiefs I worked for. I thought he had an ego the size of an elephant and a brain the size of a pea.

He asked me, "Are you putting in for the regional budget section chief job?"

I told him, "I had been thinking about it but I was torn between wanting to advance my career and not wanting to go back to commuting three hours a day and giving up so much for a little increase in pay."

He mumbled, "I can help you make that decision. I talked to Larry (The Regional Fiscal Management Officer) and he said if you put in for the job, he wouldn't hire you."

I thanked him for this inside information and as soon as he left my office, I started filling out my application for the job. I didn't want the job. I didn't want to move back to the San Francisco area, with its high cost of living. I didn't want to go back to commuting three hours per day. But I had to put the system to the test.

I sent my application in on the last day of the closing of the job announcement. It could not have been more than twenty minutes when Bob appeared. The personnel branch had told him I turned in my application for the job.

He said, "I thought you were not going to put in for the job."

I replied, "I didn't say I wasn't going to apply for the job. I told you I was not sure I wanted the job."

He said, "I told you in confidence what Larry said about not selecting you if you applied."

I said, "Thank you for the inside information, but I think I should let him make that an official decision."

I could see his discomfort. He knew me. He knew in some way he had set me off. He knew that I had something up my sleeve. He shrugged his shoulders as if to say, "I warned you," and left my office.

I waited patiently for the evaluations and ranking to be done. I received my anticipated phone call from the Regional Fiscal Management Officer (RFMO) informing me that I was in the top five candidates and he would like to interview me. I flew my plane up to the Bay Area. Of course the IRS reimbursed me for the cost of flying my plane. My wife came along. We enjoy trying out various restaurants in the city. She loved to visit the city in which she was born, raised and educated. I almost forgot about the interview. After all, I wasn't going to be selected anyway. But I showed up at the regional office on time.

I always do well in interviews. This was no different, except it felt strange sitting talking to this man about my qualifications, my insights, my ambitions when both of us knew it was just a sham. We knew each other from way back when he was a division chief at the Fresno service Center. After the interview ended I was informed that I would be notified of the outcome. We could have exchanged information on the outcome right then, but that wouldn't be proper protocol.

About the middle of the following week, I got a phone call. I was not selected. I guess I should have been devastated but I was busy. I had already started working on my complaint of discrimination. Within hours of the call telling me I had not been selected I finished it and turned it in. My allegation was that the selecting official did not select me because I was Black. He made the decision not to select me and informed my division chief of that decision before I had turned in my application for the position. I concluded that my division chief told me of the selecting officials decision to dissuade me from applying for the job. I contended that the selecting official, who is a Mormon, did not care to consider my qualifications because he had been raised in a church environment which classified black people as inferior to whites.

We went through the informal stage of the complaint process. My division chief vehemently denied telling me that the selecting official had told him I would not be hired if I put in for the job. I expected no less. After all, I had no witnesses to the conversation between the two of us. The selecting official, Larry denied telling my division chief that I would not be selected before I turned in an application.

My complaint had to go through the normal process. There was no resolution during the informal stage. An EEO investigator was sent to the Center to perform an investigation. Management was sitting back fat dumb and happy, because they knew that as long as my complaint hinged on a private conversation which I alleged took place, then I didn't have a leg to stand on. That was when I pulled my rabbit out of the hat.

I told the investigator that I wanted to include a lie detector test as part of my affidavit. I told him the IRS could select the company to do the testing and I would pay for it. I also proposed that inasmuch as the crux of this case boiled down to my word against my division chief's word, I would pay for him to take a lie detector test.

The investigator called the region and told them about my proposal. They told him that a lie detector test could not be included in the package. Also under no circumstances was the division chief going to take a lie detector test. I pointed out to the investigator that the region had erred in their assumption. If they denied me the right to include in my affidavit what I consider pertinent to my case then they are censoring me. He called them again and conveyed my thoughts.

They came back and said, "A lie detector test was not admissible in court." They were grasping at straws. I thought they might be dumb enough to take that position. I informed the investigator that this was not a court of law. Nor, was the hearing before the Equal Employment Opportunity Commission a court hearing. It is an informal hearing and the hearing officers are not judges, hence the Region's position is not valid. I insisted that I be allowed to include a lie detector test in my deposition. He called the Regional Office again and conveyed my message. I could have included this information in one of my earlier messages but I wanted to see what type of attack the Region would undertake. I looked upon this confrontation as a chess game of life.

Finally, after days of back and forth messages between the Region and the investigator the Region made the decision that I could take the lie detector test and include it in my affidavit. Understanding the way the system operates I realized that the Region did not make this decision in a vacuum. They talked to their counterparts in the National Office before conceding to my demand. Part of their decision to allow me to take the test and include it in my affidavit was so asinine that to this day, I still ask myself how could they be so ignorant? They conceded that I could take the lie detector test and include it in my affidavit. However, they said the investigator could not be present at the time I was taking the test. When the investigator told me this, I burst out laughing. He looked a little hurt and I quickly explained to him that my hilarity had nothing to do with him.

There are a lot of words which come to mind to express my feelings about that decision. Words like incredulous, insane, unbelievable or just plain dumb. Common sense and just the smallest degree of intelligence would dictate that the investigator witness my test. He was sent to Fresno to gather the facts and submit a report which would now include my lie detector test results. My testimony and everyone else he interviewed was given under oath. Now there would be an exception to this practice. My lie detector test would not be under oath. If the agency thought I was lying, and they had half a brain, this would be the perfect scenario to get rid of me or at least make a case for a suspension. If I was under oath and failed the test, wouldn't that be a case of perjury?

I took the lie detector test. Actually, lie detector test, is a misnomer in this case. The examiner pointed out to me that this was a truth affirmation test. He used the same machine which he would use in a lie detector test. I guess there is some kind of difference in interpretation between looking for a lie and affirming the truth. He assured me the results were just as accurate.

I passed the test with flying colors. An interesting part of the test was one of the last questions the examiner asked me. He asked if there was any thing I had ever done on the job to get fired. That was an easy question to answer. I said, "no." I failed the question. I was stunned. The examiner had a sly smile on his face. He explained to me that this was a validation question. He knew that anyone who had worked for the government for thirty-four years, as I had could not have worked that long without doing something to get fired. He said that if I had responded no, and passed this question he would have questioned the validity of the complete test. I was still perplexed that I had failed that question because at that moment I really did not believe that there was anything I had done on the job which could have got me fired.

Later on I thought long and hard about that validation question. The examiner was right. I dredged up a number of memories from days of long ago where I did participate in situations which could have ended my career. An example was when I was in contract administration in San Francisco. I let a few contractors buy my lunch. I didn't want to make a big deal about insisting on paying. However, I know of a case where people in my position had been fired for accepting a ride on a contractor's yacht and disciplinary actions for accepting meals and other types of gratuities from contractors. I knew better. It was poor judgement on my part. I was lucky. I looked back further and there were other things which came to mind which I would rather not mention. Let me just say they included moments of youthful poor judgement.

After the test was completed, I gave the EEO investigator a certified copy of the test results. I offered one more time to pay to have the division chief take the truth affirmation test. The investigator called the Region and was told under no circumstances would Bob, my division chief be allowed to take a lie (truth affirmation) detector test. The test cost $125. I was offering it to them for free. If the division chief had been allowed to take the test and he passed it, there would be an impasse and quite simply I would have no case.

On the other hand if he failed the test, the agency would have been forced to capitulate. They were not going to take that risk. The embarrassing question the IRS would then have to face would be what to do with two high level managers, one who failed truth affirmation test and the other who was alleged to have said he would not hire me without ever seeing my qualifications. Inasmuch, as I had passed the test they had to seriously consider the possibility that the selecting official could have told Bob that I would not be selected. Another scenario they would have to consider was that Bob may have made the whole thing up. The IRS was faced with a dilemma. There was no way they would allow any of their officials to take the truth affirmation test.

The Investigator took his completed case file back to the Regional Office in San Francisco. The waiting process began. Having been an Equal employment Opportunity officer and an Equal Employment investigator I knew the process which was going on. The EEO office reviewed the file and made recommendations to management. I sincerely believe that the agencies I worked for before going to work for the IRS attempted to find the truth and deal with it when faced with a complaint of discrimination. The IRS had no desire to find the truth. If the truth smacked them across the face they would look the other way. Their practice was to avoid dealing with the issue if possible. If someone filed a complaint which they evaluated as weak they would simply play the game and let the case drag through the system until it died on the vine. However, if they feared a case had a potential to be won by the complainant, and embarrass them, they were quick to offer some form of compromise.

I knew that my truth affirmation test results had them pulling their hair out. They were in virgin territory. They couldn't allow this case to go forward because of the potential for embarrassment. They had no other reasonable choice in order to save face. If they allowed my complaint to go forward, at each step they would be placed in a position whereas they would have to keep being faced with the results of my truth affirmation test. It stuck in their craw like a rock. I waited patiently. In a few weeks I got the phone call I expected. The Regional EEO Officer called me and offered me a compromise to get me to drop my complaint. The offer was a two month developmental detail in San Francisco to be developed for a higher position. I thought this was pretty nice a two month paid vacation in San Francisco. I went back with a counter offer. Two months in San Francisco and one month in Washington D.C. Also I was to chose the dates. They immediately accepted my counter offer. In fact to sweeten the pot they offered a fourth month. I picked the months of November and December so that my wife, a teacher, could join me during Thanksgiving and Christmas breaks. She also spent the weekends with me. I selected the month of July to go to Washington D.C. so she could join me during the summer break. I had taken my wife there for a week when I had to go there on business. She loves to travel and I had promised to take her back to Washington D.C. for a longer vacation. The reader might wonder why I didn't ask to be placed in a like position of the one I was denied? It goes back to the basic premiss which was, I didn't want to have to move to the San Francisco area. I was within three years of my planned retirement. Why would I ruin my financial status to prove a point? Then the question aries', what would I have done if I had been offered the job? I didn't think there was much of a chance of that happening. The agreement between me and the agency read as follows:

AGREEMENT

It is hereby agreed by the undersigned representative for the Western Regional Office, Internal Revenue Service (hereafter Agency) and Oscar G. Williams (hereafter complainant) that the following constitutes a full and complete settlement of the administrative complaint of discrimination filed by the complainant on January 27, 1984.

1. The Agency agrees to:
    A. Detail the complainant to the Western Regional Office Fiscal Branch (Resources Management Division) for a 30–to 60–day period. The complainant will retain his GS-12 grade while serving this detail.
    B. Detail the complainant to the National Office Fiscal Division (Planning, Finance and Research) for a 30–to 60–day period. The complainant will retain his GS-12 level while serving this detail.
    C. Provide the complainant with the two details specified above by September 1, 1985. **The purpose of these details specified above by September 1, 1985 is to further develop the complainant for positions of increasing responsibility within the Service.**

2. In consideration for the Agency's actions as outlined in (1) above, the complainant agrees:
   A. To withdraw the above-referenced complaint with prejudice.
   B. Not to institute any further legal or administrative appeals on theissues raised in the above-referenced complaint.
   C. The terms of this agreement will not establish any precedent, nor willthis agreement be used as a basis by the complainant or other personsor groups to seek or justify similar terms in any subsequent case.
   D. That this agreement does not constitute an admission by the Agency of any violation of applicable civil rights laws, or of any other federal orstate statute or regulation.
3. Complainant represents that he is voluntarily entering into thisagreement, and understands all of its provisions.
4. Both parties understand that if the Agency fails to carry out the terms of this agreement, Complainant may request, in writing, that the Regional EEO Officer reinstate the complaint at the next stage of in the processing.

Michael P. Dolan	10/10/84
Assistant Regional Commissioner (Resources Management)	Date

Oscar G. Williams	10/22/84
Complainant	Date

The stage was set. I could now take up to four months of paid vacation. When November rolled around I gave my assistant a temporary promotion to run my office; packed my bags; and was of to the Region, in San Francisco to be developed. Upon my arrival at the region I was greeted by the Assistant Regional Commissioner for Human resources. He provided the expected amount of lip service about the opportunity I had been given in this developmental assignment. He avoided saying anything about my charge of discrimination or the settlement of my case. He assigned me to work with The Regional Fiscal Management Officer (RFMO). This was part of the written agreement. It just so happens that the man in this position, was the man I alleged had discriminated against me by not hiring me because I am black. This is an excellent portrayal of the perverted manner in which the IRS management system functioned. I am sure that this was their way of rubbing the agreement in my face. However, I agreed to this strange set of circumstances because I felt that it put me in the driver's seat. If the Regional (RFMO) made one little misstep that I construed as irregular the war would be resumed. Realistically I could do no wrong. I felt this put me in a win–win position. The RFMO called me into his office. He began to go over my plan for my development for a higher level position. It consisted basically of working as a regional budget analyst. I found nothing acceptable about his proposal. I didn't go up to San Francisco to work. I went to be, "developed for positions of increasing responsibility within the service." That's what the written agreement said.

I told him, "I have budget analyst working for me. I don't see how working as a budget analyst is going to prepare me for a higher level position. This is not what I agreed to." He responded, "I'll be back," as he hightailed it out of his office. He was back in about twenty minutes. He had a new plan worked out. I liked it. **There was no work involved.** There were a number of little petty, nebulous projects such as set up the annual Regional Budget Conference and work on a plan for the Lock Box program. This is a program the IRS was exploring which contracted banks to receive taxpayer payments and deposit them without going through the IRS processing system. It was thought that this would save money. Basically what my developmental assignments boiled down to was the hidden agenda which said here are some toys to play with. If you leave us alone during your assignment, we will leave you alone.

There were no projected completion dates for the projects. I set about being developed. I called a couple of bank vice presidents and vaguely discussed the Lockbox project with them. I knew there was already an IRS task force working on the Lockbox program. I knew the chairman of the task force. His name was Frank Ramos. I called the chairman and discussed the project with him for a few minutes. I wrote a four-page report. Project completed. It's ironic how time has a way of turning back upon itself. Today in 1996 as I sit here writing this book the Fresno Bee published an article. It said:

IRS WASTED $5m,
SAY GOVERNMENT AUDITORS

Washington—The internal Revenue Service wasted nearly $5m this year by paying taxpayers to sort taxpayers checks from returns rather than doing the work itself, congressional auditors said. Under the lockbox program. the IRS in 1994 and 1995 asked participating filers who owed tax to use two envelopes—one to send their check to a bank service lockbox and the other to send their return to an IRS service center.

When I read this article, my old heart began palpitating. The paper was talking about one of my old programs, the Lockbox program which I was assigned to work on in 1984 as one of my developmental assignment. It had lost five million dollars. Could it be that if I had been better developed, while I was assigned to the Regional office, the IRS would have made money on this project?

In order to set up the budget conference, one of my developmental projects I called each of the fiscal officers, including my recently temporary promoted assistant and came up with a general consensus as to the dates and agenda. I wrote a memorandum confirming such and sent it to each office. Project completed. This project must have had some kind of hidden developmental facets which I could not fathom. A low graded clerk could have probably done the job quicker and more efficiently than I did.

My projects were finished in the first week of my two month developmental assignment in San Francisco. I knew what the game plan was and I took full advantage of it. I went and came as I chose to. Normally I would leave for lunch with some of the early lunch crowd. After they left the restaurant I would usually join another group and have a couple of more beers or martinis. I visited old acquaintances; Made plans for the evening; Picked up tickets for stage productions; and just basically did anything I thought of to entertain myself. It may seem that I was going out of my way to provoke management. In a sense this may have been true. I felt nothing but contempt for the IRS management system and those in it. I may have been unconsciously rubbing their noses in the mess they had made. In spite of my feelings for the IRS, my wife and I had a lovely expense paid vacation. She was born and raised in San Francisco. We stayed at one of the best hotels in San Francisco; frequented the best restaurants; saw a number of stage productions; and enjoyed the overall ambiance of San Francisco. One of the stage shows we saw stands out in my memory. It had just hit San Francisco. The play was Evita. It was easy to splurge on my vacation because the IRS was footing the bill for my hotel, meals and miscellaneous expenses. Of course I was also receiving my regular salary.

My wife and I flew my Cessna 172 to the East Coast. See picture of plane below. That's me on the far right. This picture was taken at the airport on Catalina Island shortly before our trip to Washington D.C. It can carry four people plus a modest amount of baggage.

Since there was just the two of us we had the back seats filled almost to the ceiling with our clothes and sporting equipment.

My plane holds forty-two gallons of fuel, of which forty is useable. The engine burns eight gallons per hour. At ten thousand feet we can cruise at about one hundred and thirty miles per hour. On our trip to Washington, D.C. we planned to stop overnight in Grand Canyon, Arizona; Wichita, Kansas (My hometown); Cincinnati, Ohio; and on into Washington, D.C. On forty gallons of useable fuel we had a maximum range of up to five hours or about six hundred and fifty miles. However, we made a number of stops at various airports along the way, because I like to stop and stretch after about three or four hours of flying. Also in consideration of the fact we were flying into unfamiliar areas I like to top off my tanks after about three or four hours of flight. You never know when you might end of lost and need that extra fuel. We could have made the trip a little quicker, but who was in a hurry? We had to do a little sight seeing here and there along the way.

Our trip to Washington, D.C. was just the way I like flying to be. It was uneventful. We were fortunate that weather was not a major problem. We ran into a little weather over the Rockies which was the northern perimeter of a storm about two hundred miles south of us. We had to climb up to eleven thousand five hundred feet to get over some of the clouds. That was really pushing my little old plane. Also we didn't have oxygen. I wouldn't have been comfortable going much higher without it. When we were leaving Cincinnati, Ohio airport we had to deviate a little south to get around a storm cell. When we arrived in the Washington, D.C. area, we landed at College Park Airport, which is right next to the University of Maryland. I left my plane there during our stay in Washington, D.C.

We stayed at my favorite hotel, the Capital Hill. It is located across the street from the new Library of congress; one block from the original Library of congress; a couple of blocks from the Capital; and the Mall. We had a suite with a kitchenette, a dining area, a living room and a separate bedroom. One of the nice features about the Capital Hill Hotel is that on one side within easy walking distance there are the touristy things to see. On the other sides it is surrounded by a lovely community of private homes; parks; cute little shops; mom and pop stores and restaurants. If I should ever move to Washington, D.C. this would be an area I would like to reside in. Below is a picture of the front of the Capital Hill Hotel. That's me leaning against the front of the hotel.

My developmental assignment in Washington, D.C. was a rerun of my assignment in San Francisco. They didn't know what to do with me. It was left up to me to entertain myself. One of my former employees worked a few doors down from my office. We often frequented the local bars for lunch, which featured topless dancers. As in San Francisco I spent a lot time studying the newspaper for entertainment and making arrangements for tickets. About the middle of our stay in Washington, D.C. we went into New York City to see a stage how on Broadway. I spent a few days watching a company filming part of a movie in the mall next door to my office. The highlight of me and my wife's Washington, D.C. trip was the July fourth celebration on the mall. Since we were just two blocks away my wife and our friends got there early. We spread our blanket just below the Capital and munched on cheese and crackers with a Toast of wine to Leonard Bernstein who was entertaining us that evening.

I call my wife a professional tourist. She has been to the Orient, Europe and most places in between. Each morning before I left for the office she showed me her touring itinerary for the day. I hate being a tourist. I thanked God that I had to go to the office to be developed. We were fortunate in meeting a group of people who played tennis at a local park every evening. Each day after being developed, and my wife's touring we went to the park and played with them. When they found out that we were from the west coast it became a friendly rivalry between the east and west coast.

I have been describing all of the fun we had, and it might be assumed that I forgot to mention my development. Unless the IRS has discovered a form of Osmoses management development, there is nothing to tell concerning my development. Finally my three month developmental assignment (vacation) came to and end. Common sense would dictate that during the process of development there would be periods of consoling as to my developmental progress. Not one word was uttered during the three months as to how my development was going.

One would certainly expect that at the end of the developmental assignment I would get some kind of evaluation. It never happened. The IRS paid a minimum of twenty thousand tax dollars to develop me. This includes my wages and benefits for three months, travel and per diem expenses for three months and the temporary promotion of my assistant. Not one word was uttered as to whether I was fully developed, half developed or not developed at all. Nor was their any type of discussion as to what I had been developed to do. Was I now developed enough to be an assistant regional commissioner or maybe I was so developed I could just move up to regional commissioner. It should be pretty obvious that the IRS had no intention of developing me for anything. They bought me off in order to get me to drop my discrimination complaint. Their buyout of me served their need to save face.

I didn't take the fourth month because of personal commitments. Believe it or not there is a limit to how much fun one can have. After all with my three month developmental assignment coupled with my normal month of vacation I had been away from the old homestead for over four months.

My wife and I were going to fly a leisurely northern course going back to Fresno from Washington, D.C. However, we felt a little tired and pressed for time. She wanted to get back and start preparing for the next school year and I just wanted to sit still for a little while and let life catch up with me. Rather than heading north as planned we basically flew back the same way we had gone to Washington, D.C. One thing sticks in my mind about the trip home. We stopped in St Louis Missouri for our first overnight stay. I turned on the television to catch up on the news. All of the stations were showing the aftermath of the DC-10 which had just crashed in Dallas while landing. All onboard were killed. It was a weather related accident. I sat there looking at the fire and carnage. I asked myself, "who do you think you are, flying your little plane across the United States?'

The next day when I called in for a weather check en route to Kansas city and to Liberal, Kansas, the FAA weatherman suggested that I do not fly into the Kansas City area because of thunderstorms coming through the area all day.

He suggested I go down south and go into Kansas from the east. I took a southern route through Springfield, Missouri. We hit some rain, but not too much turbulence before we got to Liberal, Kansas. As we were making our way through the inclement weather, I couldn't help but think about the DC-10 which weather had destroyed yesterday. I wasn't looking forward to challenging the Rockies the next day. However, the following day when we got to the Rockies it was so clear you could see forever. It was a moment of serene enhancement as we floated between the towering peaks. God was with us all of the way home.

There is the very positive side to this whole scenario. The IRS provided me and my wife with a type of vacation I could not afford unless I happened to hit the LOTTO. I sincerely thank Bob, my former division chief for making it possible for us to have a three month expense paid vacation. It would not have been possible without him.

Other Sporting Activities

Bob also provided other sporting activities. I called them sporting activities because they were competitive. One uneventful day I sat in my usual position in my office, feet on desk, reared back, looking at the ceiling when a close friend of mine, Rob Marion the Public affairs Officer came into my office. His body language said he was not a happy camper. He sat down and handed me a memorandum. He asked me to read it. I read it and started laughing before I got halfway through. He looked hurt and confused.

The memorandum was from Bob. It told Rob what a bad and inefficient person he was. Before Rob said anything I pulled a file out of my cabinet and said, "read this. He looked at the title. The title of the file is, "Dumbshit." I called it the Dumbshit file because it consisted of a number of memorandums Bob had written me telling me what a dumbshit I was. It included my written responses to each of his memorandums. The first of his memos was one page long. My response was two pages long. In my response I pointed out flaws in his perception and provided factual information to fill in where he had made general assumptions.

In his second memorandum which came a few months after the first there was the same general accusations. The only difference was this memorandum was two pages long. I wrote him a proper response. My response was three pages long. I ended it as I had my first by questioning our communication system which had deteriorated to having to write memorandums back and forth. I suggested that he and I should sit down and talk theses things out if there were things which concerned him. I thought about it, but I didn't mention to him that this unfounded harassment could lead to another expenses paid vacation for me.

A few months later came the third and last memorandum. It was four pages long. By the way the memorandum pages were increasing one might assume that I and my office were going to the dogs. I like the ending of this memorandum. Bob must have thought about my comment in my last memorandum to him where I mentioned the futility of writing memos back and forth. He ended this third memo by saying, "Rather than spending your time writing me a memorandum in response to what I have said, I suggest you spend the time correcting the problems."

When I could finally stop myself from laughing I wrote Bob a six page memorandum. Again I pointed out the facts, as opposed to his perception. I ended it with, "It's a shame how our communication system has failed." I didn't receive any more memorandums from Bob. I was sorry he stopped writing me because it would have only taken a couple of more memorandums and Bob would have got the IRS to send me on another expense paid vacation.

My friend Rob read through my, "Dumbshit file." He said, "I didn't know he wrote you anything like this." I said, "It wasn't worth mentioning to anyone." I then went on to explain to him that Bob considered himself documenting me. My written rebuttals threw him off track because his accusations had been defused. I warned my friend that he should not let the charges in Bob's memorandum go unanswered in writing, because later on down the line that becomes documentation. It will be too late to say that wasn't true at a later date because things in writing have a way of appearing to have been etched in stone, if they are not dealt with. I pointed out that going unchallenged these accusations could become grounds for Bob to take some kind of disciplinary action. My friend had a smile on his face and a bounce to his walk as he left my office to go write a memo to Bob.

I sometimes look back, with a smile on my face as I wonder how Bob ever thought of taking on a pro like me when he started writing me memorandums. He was out of his league. In a way I'm glade he did because it helped me fill some of my leisure time.

First Class Baggage

Early in my tenure with the IRS, I was sitting around reading policy statements. One in particular got my attention. This policy provided that a person could be authorized first class air travel if he had some kind physical characteristic which required more than the room in coach provided. I didn't do anything at that moment with this tidbit of information, other than to store it away in my mental nice to know file. However, with time things can change. After a few years I had become disenchanted with the organization. I didn't pass up any chance to pull their chain.

I wrote a memorandum, through channels to the regional commissioner requesting approval for me to travel first class on my business trips. My justification for the request was based upon the fact that I am six feet seven inches tall, and suffer considerable discomfort flying in the coach section because of the limited space. I was surprised when I received an approval memorandum without having to go to war over the issue.

I traveled all over the country in first class doing IRS business. I always tried to ensure I got a large airliner like the Boeing 747, Douglas DC-10 or other similar type aircraft because they had all of the first class amenities. Following are many of the cities I traveled to:

San Francisco. I often flew into San Francisco. I always flew on a Boeing 737. Since we were so close to San Francisco I only got a couple of free drinks during the flight.

Detroit. I made a number of trips to payroll center in Detroit. On these trips I always flew in a large jet such as a DC-10, DC-8 or a Boeing 707.These aircraft had all of the appointed luxury items included in first class air travel.

Hawaii. I flew in a Boeing 747 to and from Hawaii. Even though the IRS paid for my first class fair I had to pay for my wife and sons first class fair. It was still a deal because my family got free lodging in my IRS sponsored quarters at the Hawaiian Hilton hotel over looking Wakiki beach. On the way back all of the travelers were tired and they stayed on the main deck, of the first class section and slept or watched movies. I went up stairs to the lounge (the bubble just behind the cockpit on a 747). There was one other person there. Turns out he was an Engineer who worked for Boeing and had gone to Hawaii to tune one of the engines on our plane. A stewardess came up and asked us what we would like to drink. I responded brandy and my traveling companion asked for bourbon.

She brought me an unopened fifth of brandy. She gave the other guy an unopened bottle of bourbon. We sat there, watching the clouds passing below us, sipped our liquor and exchanged some long stories. During the whole trip to San Francisco the two of us had the lounge to ourselves. When we arrived in San Francisco much of the contents of our bottles were gone. To the laughter of my family I had to help my new found friend find his gate to Seattle.

Memphis. My trip to Memphis had a sort of funny side to it. My division chief came along on the trip. There I sat in the first class section of the 707 and my chief was back in coach, with the poor people. Before we left I told him I loved him like a brother, but I wasn't going to give up my first class seating and sit in coach with him.

Seattle. Large jet airliner. All of the amenities.

Portland. Large jet. All of the amenities.

Boise. Small jet, drinks and status.

Philadelphia. Large jet, all of the amenities.
Washington, D.C. Large jet all of the amenities.
Chicago. Large jet all of the amenities.

As the old saying goes, "All good things must come to an end." After a few years of flying first class all over the country I received a memorandum from the regional commissioner revoking my first class travel privileges. The reason for this action was a change in the policy of the IRS because it gave the wrong image to the public. I almost took this as a personal affront. I had begun to look at my privilege as my right. I often look back and ask myself was I the one who killed the fatted calif? Invariably you talk to your fellow travelers when you are flying. The usual things you learn during these conversations are where a person is from, why he is traveling and who he works for. I always saw the eyebrows raise when I told my fellow travelers I worked for the IRS and I was on a business trip. I never told them I had some kind of special disposition in order to travel first class. That would have taken away from the image. There I was flying all over the country, implying that we IRS executives flew first class. How long do you think it took for this information to get to the treasury Department or the hierarchy in the IRS? Needless to say my business travel seemed to decline after I lost my first class seat.

Too Much Work–Too Little Pay

In the mud eighties I began the process of what today is known as downsizing. At that time I was responsible for: budget preparation and execution; timekeeping; payroll;

the quality assurance program for the Forms Distribution Program; the perfection of vendor invoices for payment; and performing management analysis studies. My desire to downsize came as a culmination of a number of things. One was an attempt to move the Procurement Unit from the Facilities Management Branch to my office. That would add six more people and due to the personalities involved it would add six hundred problems. .

After I was approached about this move by Bob, I went to the Personnel Branch and told them to look into their crystal ball and tell me if this would entail a grade increase from a GS-12 to a GS-13. They said no. The level of responsibility would not increase sufficiently to warrant a grade increase. I fought the move tooth and nail. I think the winning ploy was that I pointed out that throughout the IRS this unit was in the Facilities Management Branch. This meant my office would not be in the normal cycle of communication. If something important didn't get to me and there was a screw up who would be to blame. This turned out to be the same ploy I used to get timekeeping and Payroll transferred to the Personnel Branch.

Bob considered my argument. He decided not to move the unit. I think his decision had a lot to do with survival. I am sure that deep down inside he knew that if this mis-communication I spoke of didn't happen by accident It could occur in other ways. In the long run who would be to blame for a major mis-communication. It wouldn't be me because I warned him of the possible consequences in writing.

After that little fiasco of warding off further growth in my organization, I got to thinking and looking around. There were a lot of people making just as much money or more than me who had for less responsibility. I decided that it was time to balance my responsibility with my pay. I decided to downsize. When my management analyst position became vacant I simply did not fill it. I decided not to do anymore management analysis studies. The ones we had done over the years were an absolute waste because few if any of the IRS managers knew what they were reading.

The move of the Tax Forms Distribution program to Sacramento eliminated my quality assurance program and eliminated two positions. The real headache was time-keeping and payroll. I started trying to get these programs moved to the Personnel Branch. I wasn't having very much success. In fact I would not have been successful if for a small moment of opportunity in which the Personnel Branch chief and my division chief, Bob had a small tiff. At that fertile moment, with my friendly persuasion I got Bob to move timekeeping and payroll to personnel. There went eighteen people and a multitude of headaches.

I was left with two budget analyst, an invoice perfection clerk and my secretary. I even got rid of my branch chief status desk. If I had anything to write I did it on a little rollout shelf on one of my file cabinets. When my division chief visited with me after I had disposed of my desk he commented about how empty my office looked. My response was I liked a lot of room to roam around when I was thinking. I had plenty of time in the last four years of my career to contemplate my naval and a lot of room to do it in.

The irony of this whole scenario is that after I left the organization my old job was upgrades to a GS-13. One of the good old boys from the regional office was put in it.

My assistant who had received a promotion to my job retained her promotion but was reclassified as a budget analyst. The new Fiscal Officer was now a GS-13. Keep in mind that this increase in grade occurred after I had stripped the office of most of the it's programs. If this seems a little odd, a few years later the incumbent Fiscal Officer left and another good old boy was placed in the position. The name of my old job was changed to Comptroller, and the grade was increased to a GS-14. The reason given for this increase is because the Procurement Unit was moved into the Fiscal Office. This is the same Procurement unit which the Personnel Branch had told me could not increase my grade from a GS-12 to a GS-13. This was before I downsized and got rid of almost all of my office. Something is at work here which defies my ability to understand.

I realize that the mentor system has some bearing upon grade. That's the real world. I was not the most popular person with management in the IRS. This could account for one grade differential. If I had been a company man there is no doubt in my mind that my position would have been one grade higher. But two grades? Was I that unpopular or could other factors be at work. The two good old boys who had the benefit of promotions in my old position are white. I am black. Maybe like some of the Texaco black employees, I was stuck to the bottom of the pan and just couldn't shake loose. Then again maybe this was payback time. This is the way the IRS decided to balance the books for the time they hired me as their token black, when they should have promoted one of their two very well qualified white employees who were vying for the job.

The reason for the two grade increase of my old job will never be known, unless we could put the IRS officials who executed the actions on a lie detector machine. What is the chance of that ever happening? Getting an IRS official near a lie detector machine would be like trying to push a camel through the eye of a needle or salvaging an ice cube in hell.

Hot Things

During the first couple of years of our operation I constantly heard complaints from managers about how our employees dressed. To me they dressed like people dressed everywhere. Then I realized where the complaints were coming from. They were coming from the Ogdinites (people hired from the Ogden Utah Service Center). For those of you who don't know this is Mormon territory. They couldn't adjust to tank tops, cutoffs and flip flops. They kept trying to get management to set a dress code. At least seventy to eighty percent of the cadre of supervisors hired to start the center came from the Ogden Service Center, which is located in Ogden Utah.

In Ogden there was a dress code. On one of my business trips to Ogden, which I tried to keep at a minimum, I invited myself to a fashion show the center was holding to show managers what was not appropriate dress for employees. The dress code show only included women. Apparently men know how to dress in Utah. The women modeled tank tops, cutoffs and flip flops. These were example of dress which the supervisors were instructed to watch for and send any employee home who came to work in this type of dress. If this show had been in California the supervisors would have had to go send home half of the work force. The acceptable dress styles looked a lot like how beaver's mother dressed in, "Leave it to Beaver." Back in Fresno the Ogdinites were still trying to force some kind of dress code on the populace.

I got kind of tired hearing the Ogdinites (people from Ogden Utah) complaining and watching the directors staff wringing their hands trying to respond to the demands. I decided to make a statement. When I worked for the Air force in San Bernardino California, at Norton Air Force Base the Air Force officers were allowed to wear summer dress uniforms to work. Summer dress consisted of a short sleeve shirt, no tie and walking shorts. I thought this made a lot of sense. I bought some walking shorts. I wore them to the office during the summer months. However, I did bow to a little custom by adding a white shirt and a tie to my ensemble. I found that I was not the only civilian adopting this form of summer dress. I ran into a couple of other civilians in their walking shorts.

Fresno is a desert valley city just like San Bernardino where the temperatures sore into the hundreds in the summer. I decided to bring the IRS into the twentieth century. In May of 1972 I shopped around and found a pair of walking shorts. One hot morning I donned my walking shorts, a white shirt, tie and a vest and trekked off to the IRS service center. I purposely went very early. I went to the cafeteria and had a coffee. The cafeteria began to fill up. I left for my office about ten minutes before work was scheduled to begin. When I got up from my seat in the cafeteria there was a buzz of conversation, people were pointing some were laughing. I knew what was happening.

I sauntered out of the cafeteria as if nothing was unusual. When I walked through the central building of our five building complex, I had to walk through an area which had hundreds of data transcribers and clerks. They were primarily women. They stood up at their work stations and hooted and whistled. This was the reaction I expected. That's why I went early to avoid disrupting work. By the time I got back to my office the news had preceded me. The photographer from our Public Affairs Office was there to take a picture of me. He took a picture of me and my secretary, Vickie Smilie staged to look as if we were discussing work. See picture below.

I got calls from a number of branch chiefs in the outlying buildings who suddenly wanted to talk over some financial matters. These were unusual request. Normally they didn't want to talk to me about finance because I usually was talking about overruns or cutting resources. It was evident that the outlying branches had heard about my walking shorts and wanted a live presentation. I went to visit each of the branch chiefs who called me. When I got to their offices, I told them I knew why I had been called to meet with them on some mysterious financial matter. Each of them confessed that they wanted their people to get a look at the Fiscal Officer in his walking shorts. The work force in a service center is predominately women. In each branch they had a ball hooting and whistling.

When I returned to my office after making the rounds there was a message from the director asking me to drop in on him. I went over to his office. His office was about thirty feet from mine. Both the director and assistant director were in the directors office. When I walked in the director Lynn Semrick, said, "so that's what all the talk is about." I sat down. I said, "It gets pretty hot here, I thought I'd pull and old pair of my walking shorts out that I used to wear when I worked in San Bernardino. I can't imagine what all of the fuss is about." The assistant director, Bud Pearson said, "those aren't walking shorts they're hot pants." Both the director and I got a good laugh at that comment. The director and I chatted for a while. I let the fact enter into the conversation that I had let the ladies have their look throughout the center and did not intend to go back out in the working areas.

When I got back to my office I found that the word had spread that I had been called to the directors office. While I was in the directors office the Ogdinites were chanting, "Send him home. Send him home." When some of my acquaintances called and asked what the director had said I told them he and the assistant liked my attire so well they were thinking of making it mandatory dress for summer wear.

I had not planned to repeat the performance with the walking shorts. I felt the staid IRS had been tested enough.

I put my shorts away and forgot about them. However, about a week later I got a call from an acquaintance of mine, Vern Deason, a regional analyst on the staff of the regional commissioner. Vern said, "Oscar, the RC (Regional Commissioner) saw your picture in the Fresno newspaper and he is pissed. He called me into his office and asked, "what the hell is going on down there in Fresno?" Vern was giving me a friendly warning that there might be some stuff coming from the top on this. I thanked Vern for his call, but I couldn't help asking Vern if the RC didn't have anything better to do than to sit around looking at pictures?

I also got calls from a couple of National offices acquaintances when the paper hit the national office. After the commotion died down the Fresno Directors staff finally came up with a dress policy. I was pleasantly surprised that the Ogdinites didn't prevail in their attempt to have everyone sent directly to hell if they didn't dress to suit them. The dress policy simply stated that an employee must be sent home if he/she wore clothing which was dangerous or disrupted production. I don't believe that my walking pants demonstration caused the directors staff to come to a decision. But there is no way they could have a meeting concerning dress codes and not mention my walking shorts.

An Earful

When I turned fifty my wife asked me what I wanted for my birthday. I told her I would like to have an earring. My request surprised her, but she thought that it was a great idea. Off we went to the jewelers to have my ear

pierced. The right ear, not the left. I have always thought
that if you want to be different then don't be the same as
everyone else. The vast number of men who wore earrings
in nineteen eighty three wore them in their left ear. They
were concerned with the old homophobic wive's tale about
men being gay if they wore an earring in their right ear. Not
being homophobic or gay and wanting a change of pace, I
told the jeweler to zap my right ear. He seemed a little hesi-
tant and asked, "the right ear?" "Yes," I said and the deed
was done.

I was aware that there were not a lot of IRS male
managers wearing earrings. In fact I had not seen any in
the thirteen years I had worked for the IRS. There were a
lot of surprised looks when I showed up with my earring.
I wore a diamond stud. People looked but no one said
anything, except for my immediate staff. One of my budget
analyst wore an earring, in his left ear of course. My staff
had a field day with my earring. They had questions like
"Isn't there something you want to tell us?", or, "didn't
you get the wrong ear pierced? I got a kick out of their
unveiled hilarity.

Finally my division chief, Bob couldn't hold back the
question any longer. One day I was in his office. We had
concluded our business. I was about to leave when he said,
"Wait a minute Oscar. Sit down." He slouched down into
his chair into what I had coined the, Bullshit position. He
scooted his chair over to my chair and slapped his hand on
my knee. I guess this was his way of saying I was okay. He
asked, "Oscar, what does the earring mean?" I had my
chance and I blew it. I should have responded with something like, "I love you Bob." I smiled at him as I was

thinking and all I could come up with was, "I have a thing for diamonds." I got up and left him slouched in his chair.

I didn't miss the next opportunity to have a little fun with my earring. On one of my business trips to the regional office, in San Francisco I dropped in on the Analysis Staff to chat. I knew most of them because I had worked in the office for a short time. I knew the news of my earring had preceded me. I had received a couple of calls from acquaintances both in the region and from the national office inquiring, "is it true?" When I walked into the analysis office one of the analyst across the room hailed me with, "Hey Oscar, what's with this earring thing?" He was a good old boy, ex-marine, macho, the whole nine yards. Everyone was looking at me for a reaction. I yelled back across the room, "kiss me and I'll tell you." The other analyst in the office rolled on their desk in laughter. The inquisitive analyst's face turned beet red and he suddenly gave the papers on his desk all of his attention.

Like all old business the newness of the earring wore off. I only got surprised reactions and sideways glances when I went to offices which I did not usually visit.

A Thousand Words

I have heard that a picture is worth a thousand words. In 1985 I had pretty well formed an opinion of the IRS management system. It was not a good opinion. The deceit in the system, like the destruction of thousands of taxpayer inquires, the lack of sincerity in resolving EEO complaints, the practice of awarding themselves fat bonuses for just doing their job had soured me completely on the IRS's management philosophy. I often voiced my opinion of the system but I needed a visual reminder. Something that silently spoke for me. I painted a picture. It is an oil painting. The canvass is eighteen by twenty-four inches. I put it in a nice gold frame and hung it in my office.

I named the picture, "Pigs." (See picture below).

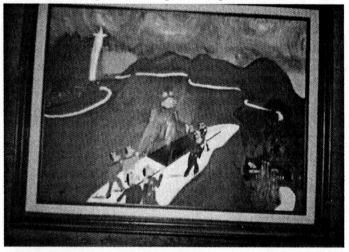

In the lower right-hand corner is a building in a valley being consumed by flames. This is a representation of the Fresno Service Center in a burning chaos. A winding road leads from the valley floor, winds up into the mountains and leads to a city in the upper left hand-corner. The city sits next to a bay with a distinctive tower in the center of it, The Trans America Building. The Golden gate spans the bay. The city is San Francisco, where the Western Regional IRS office is located. In the center of the picture are seven human forms, in clowns clothing carrying a throne chair.

All of the figures have pig faces with a protruding bright red tongues. The number of pigs carrying the throne chair equal the number of pigs, "oops," division chiefs on the directors staff. On the throne chair is the big pig. It is no coincidence that the big pig and the director both had a mustache and wore glasses. The painting portrays the abandonment of the center by its leaders the director and his staff as we all burn in hell they have created. This painting hung in my office for three years until I retired.

Over the years many people, including the people it depicted studied the painting and tried to guess its meaning. I would only tell them the name of the painting, "Pigs." No one came close to figuring it out until one day a section chief in the personnel office, Ellen Moridan began to get close to the truth. I always knew she was too bright to work for the IRS. She asked me if I would tell her if her analysis was correct or not. I told her I would not. She studied the picture for a number of minutes. She had seen it before but for some reason it drew her attention on this day. She began guessing. It was eerie and a little unsettling because she was hitting the nail right on the head. She guessed correctly that the burning building was the service center. She said, "The people in the center of the painting have something to do with the service center and they were going to San Francisco." That was the closes anyone came to figuring out what the painting represented. She then asked, "Am I close?" I just smiled at her and said, "Some day before I retire I'll tell you what it represents."

The reason I told no one what it represented was because there would have probably been a confrontation between the director and his staff and me as to the picture being removed. There would have been another protracted fight between me and the organization. I think the end result of that would have been the removal of all pictures and postures from walls within the center. I was satisfied to have made my artistic statement. This painting now hangs in my garage. I would be glade to donate it to the IRS at no cost. All they have to do is ask.

Vallay Girls

Talk about fun things. Wow. Imagine thousands of California Valley girls all together under one roof. There were all shapes, colors, tall and short. They were all California Valley girls. With the exceptions of rock concerts you could not find a collection like we had in the Fresno, California Service Center. This is the center of the San Joaquin Valley where, "Valley Girls," originated. From the bottom to the top of the organization there was a feeding frenzy as the sexual predators chose their victims. Things got so hot that in one of our staff meetings, our division chief told the chief of security to have the guards on the night shift walk throughout the parking lot and watch for people frolicking in campers and cars. For some reason this activity bothered some of the night employees who didn't or couldn't participate. I can only assume that the complainers were too old, too ugly or Mormon.

We had some classic affairs. The oddest I think was the affair between the Chief of the Management Staff and one of his analyst. This thing heated up to the point that at a weekly staff meeting the chief proudly told his staff that he and his analyst lover were going to divorce their respective spouses and marry one another. At this point in time both of them had neglected to inform their spouses. After the announcement one of the not very bright analyst in the staff meeting offered his congratulations. The intelligent ones sat there with their mouths wide open in astonishment. It's one thing to air your dirty linen, but it's another thing to flap it in peoples faces.

The guy who offered the congratulations is a complete dummy. I can call him that because he worked for me on a developmental detail. He was always out of step with reality. The news of this impending un-wedding and re-wedding spread quickly. It just so happens that the husband of the analyst worked in the center. He worked in Criminal Investigation. The quirky thing here was he legally carried a gun. When the news got to him through the grapevine that he was soon to become a divorcee, allegedly he took off to the local tavern and got bombed. A couple of friends went with him to help him through the crises. While he was at the bar he was alleged to have threatened to blow the brains out of the Chief of Management Staff. His friends were able to talk him out of it and got him home safely.

When the news got to the Chief of the Management Staff's wife, that she was going to be dropped, she allegedly told him if he went through with his plans he and his sweetie wouldn't have a pot to piss in. I had met the wife a couple of times. She was a business woman and she seemed like a no nonsense person who could deal with a problem pretty forcefully. Soon love flew out the window and the guy took an early retirement. The analyst got a divorce and a transfer to another office.

During this period of lust and love in the center a close acquaintance of mine a branch chief in The facilities Management Branch found himself a pauper before he knew what hit him. He and his, "Valley Girl," his secretary had a thing going. She misunderstood the situation. She thought it was love when it was the other word. Lust. The secretary told her husband she wanted a divorce to marry my buddy. The husband called the branch chief's wife and clued her in. There were two ugly divorcees. A few weeks after the fur had settled I was playing tennis with my buddy. He was staying at what we refereed to as the recently divorced apartment complex. For some reason the recently single IRS ex-husbands, seemed to gravitate to this particular apartment complex after the axe had fallen. My buddy told me he was paying his ex-wife, and two children half of his salary. I thought this isn't too bad. A single guy doesn't need a lot of money. He went on to tell me his wife was still so upset about what happened that when she found out that he was going to go to the local university at night for an advanced degree on the G.I. Bill she had her lawyer file for half of the tuition fee. I have heard the saying, "If you play you must pay," but how much?

"Valley Girls," can really mess up a guy's mind. Being around all of these girls sent one division chief over the edge. The problem was the poor guy was surrounded by Valley Girls all day at work, but he didn't have one of his own. This apparently drove him to desperation. It seems that during his off duty hours he started making obscene calls to a branch secretary. He disguised his voice. Even though the branch secretary spoke to him on the phone during the day when he called her office to talk to her boss, she didn't recognize the caller who was harassing her at home. This must have got good to him because he made a bad mistake. He made a couple of calls to his own secretaries home. Even though he disguised his voice, she recognized it and reported him to Inspection. During the investigation it also came out that he had been seen driving around the apartment complex where the branch secretary lived. When he was confronted with the charges he immediately took an early retirement.

I happened to get in the middle of one of those affairs which went astray. Another Chief of the Management Analysis Staff had an affair with one of his analyst. This was the second Chief of the Management Analyst staff to engender a relationship with one of the female analyst. This guy was married. The analyst was single. They made no secret they were a pair. Things went along fine for a couple of years then things seemed to go sour. She broke off the relationship. The problem was he still had the hots for her. The situation became untenable. It was causing unrest in the organization. The guy was transferred to a management position in the Regional office. The woman was transferred to my office to fill a vacant management analyst position I had. The transfer of the guy to the Regional office was not a promotion, but in a sense it was a raise in status. In my opinion the transfer of the woman to my office was a downgrade in status. As in many cases like this, the guy gets a pat on the back, the woman gets screwed.

She had been working for me about two months. One day she came into my office. She said she had a problem. She didn't know what to do about it. She said her ex-boss and ex-lover had been calling her on the job, and at home, trying to pressure her back into the relationship. This was in the late seventies, long before sexual harassment was heard of. I told her I thought I could help resolve the problem of him bothering her at work, but there was nothing I could do about him calling her at home. As soon as she left my office I picked up the phone and dialed her ex-lover in his Regional Office. His secretary put me through to him. He started out,

"Hi, Oscar!" I ignored his greeting and got right to the point.

I said, "My employee told me that you have been calling her here on the job on personnel business. There was silence on the other end. I continued, "My phones are for Government business. If you call her in my office again on personnel business, my next phone call will be to your boss." There was still silence.

I asked, "Do you understand me?"

He said, Yes," and hung up. I got more pleasure from that call than if I had hit the jackpot. I had not told my employee but I had never liked her ex-lover. He reminded me of a sleazy used car dealer. A phony. Just looking at him or listening to him talk used to annoy me. It had nothing to do with my employee's affair with him. I just didn't like him. I didn't like the way he dressed, talked and I couldn't stand the silly plastered grin he always had on his face.

It gave me great deal of pleasure to inform my employee of my phone call. She thanked me profusely. I told her to let me know the moment he called her at work again. I waited for a few weeks. Nothing seemed to be happening. I thought maybe she was too embarrassed to tell me he had called again. One day I asked her if there had been anymore calls. She said, "No. None." He had not even called her at home. She again thanked me for my intervention. She was a good employee. A hard worker. She worked for me for about a year. She got a new job and a promotion in the National Office in Washington, D.C. I think she deserved it. A couple of years after I retired, I attended a going away party for one of my old IRS cronies. My former analyst had flown in from Washington, D.C. to attend it. She introduced me to her new husband. I am very happy for her.

A guy has to guard himself against Valley girls. But I can't help but mention how California girls can get to a guy. We had a guy transfer in from our Washington, D.C. office. He became our Regional Budget Section chief. He was the quiet type, but apparently an observant one. After a short time in San Francisco he announced he was going back to Washington, D.C. However, he neglected to tell anyone that he was taking a California girl trophy with him. She happened to be married but that was solved with a divorce. He, his California trophy and her daughter were off to Washington, D.C.

My Last Big Ha-Ha

In 1987 I had unofficially announced my forthcoming retirement in June of 1988, the moment I turned fifty-five. I could not officially turn in my retirement papers because the Civil Service Regulations doesn't allow a person to submit them earlier than thirty days before the date of retirement. Even though I couldn't turn my paper work in, I had my secretary type them a year in advance of my retirement date. I had the Personnel Branch review them a number of times to ensure there would be no last minute screw ups. These things happen. We had a branch chief retire a few years earlier. She moved to Utah after she had retired. When the Civil Service Commission did a review of her files, they found she was short a period of time for retirement. The IRS took her back on board at the Ogden service Center in order for her to get the necessary time for her to correct the problem. I don't think the IRS would do that for me. I'm sure they would just say, "Too bad sucker." After I had the Personnel people review my records until they got tired of me, I put my papers in my file cabinet and waited.

In 1987 the position of Regional Equal Employment Opportunity Officer became vacant. I applied for the job. Everyone was shocked because I had made it no secret that I was going out the door the day I turned fifty-five. Many people asked me if I had changed my mind about retirement. I told them it's possible, but don't bet on it. What I didn't tell them was I had a hidden agenda. All I wanted was to get an interview for the job. Since this position was on the staff of the Regional Commissioner it meant he would be in on the interview. I relished the idea that this would give me a chance to tell the regional commissioner what I thought about his failed Equal Employment Opportunity (EEO) program. I had no fear of getting the job. Like most high profile jobs the unofficial word was already on the grapevine that a woman, the EEO Officer in the Los Angeles District was slated to get the job. Because of my experience as an EEO officer in another agency, I was ranked in the top five. I just wanted to get an interview. I got my wish. I received a call from the regional office informing me of my scheduled interview date. I immediately went to the facilities Management Branch and checked out a tape recorder.

I hopped into my plane (a Cessna 172) and flew up to the Bay Area. I was ushered into the Regional Commissioner's office. The regional commissioner and one of his assistant regional commissioners (ARC) were in the office. Also the National Office Equal Employment Opportunity Officer, from Washington, D.C. was there. I was offered a seat and a cup of coffee. I declined the coffee. I sat down and placed my briefcase on the coffee table which sat between us. I took the tape recorder out of my briefcase and sat it on the table. The ARC and the National Office EEO Officer recoiled back in their chairs. One would have thought I had placed a rattle snake on the table. I asked them if I could record the interview. I said, "I would like to use the tape later to critique the interview."

The three of them sat there looking at each other. They didn't exchange any words. Finally the regional commissioner said, "We would prefer that you did not tape the interview. If you want a critique we would be glade to provide one at a later date." How did he know that the group had this preference? Obviously they had some kind of subliminal communication system to which I was not privy. I placed the tape recorder in my briefcase and closed it. I left my briefcase sitting on the table. I knew that even though I was told not to tape the interview, they could not be sure I had not turned the tape recorder on before coming into the room. I am sure there was this underlying feeling because of the surreptitious glances the briefcase kept getting. What was the underlying fear which made them not want to have the interview taped? The IRS is not big on innovation but here was a chance for them to break in a new concept of interviewing. What could be better for the interviewee than to have a tape to play over and over and assess his answers, presentation voice pitch etc.? What kind of a hidden agenda did they have that caused them to almost panic at the sight of a tape recorder?

The interview started. We went through the normal routine. They asked me if I was familiar with the position? I told them I had previously held such a position in another agency. At the end of the interview I was asked if I had any questions or comments. Boy, did I have comments. My whole reason for putting in for the job was to get to this point. This was my chancre to tell the top dog what I thought of his EEO program and he had to listen. In addition to that the top dog from Washington was here.

I told them about my being hired to meet a quota. I told them how I was being given an annual award of one thousand dollars because of the color of my skin. I told them that these acts were personally demeaning. I told them about the necessity for minorities to form an EEO Ad hoc Committee in the Fresno, Service Center in order to thwart the practices of racism. I told them how the numbers game, hiring quotas of minorities had backfired in the districts and last, but not least I reminded the Regional commissioner of the discriminatory practices at the Ogden Service Center whereas when white managers went to the center on business they were given passes to the private clubs in the area. When black managers went to the center on business they were not offered passes to the private clubs.

The reason I say I reminded him is because he had been to the Ogden Service Center a number of times. He could not have missed seeing the system I described. My closing comment was, "If I should be hired to fill the position I will take the program from the paper where it now exist and make it a reality. Managers will be held accountable for managing the program rather than filling quotas. The game Playing would stop."

When I stopped talking the three of them sat there staring at me as if I was something alien. I have to give the Regional Commissioner some credit for being a politician. He didn't show a lot of body language. However, his crony and the National Office visitor looked as if they had just seen a horror movie. They kept looking back and forth between the Regional Commissioner and me, expecting at any moment that he would point his finger at me and I would be destroyed by a bolt of lightening. After a prolonged silence the Regional Commissioner began to defend the IRS's EEO program. I had my say. I sat there quietly until he had finished his defense of the system. When he was finished he asked if I had any additional comments. I informed him that I didn't. He told me they were glade I came to the interview and that I would be notified of the selection. After I had left I remembered that I intended to tell them who the selectee was going to be. In fact as predicted the woman in Los Angeles got the job. As I left the Regional Commissioner's Office his secretary gave me a phone message from my division chief, back in Fresno. She said he had called just after I went in for the interview. I called him. The first thing out of his mouth was,

"You didn't tape the interview did you?"

I said, "They wouldn't let me."

He commented, "Oscar, only you would try something like this."

He went on to say that when he heard what I planned to do he called immediately to try and stop me. It really wasn't important but It's kind of funny that to this day I never did ask him who tipped him off. I had only told a few people what I was going to do.

Management Foibles

Management implies leadership. I believe that it is implicit that this be by directing and by example. There were three things which stood out in my tenure with the IRS which depicts the style and nature of their management philosophy. One facet is the, "Us and them syndrom." The us being the IRS and the them being everyone else, i.e., the public the Congress and the Executive Office. The second part of the philosophy is to intimidate and crush anyone or organizations which the IRS considers a threat to its authority. This applies to IRS non-management employees as well as outsiders. The third thing which management concerns itself about is image. Image is everything to the IRS. They will withhold information, lie to the media, the Executive Office and the Congress in order to keep their image intact. Even though the Congress and the Executive Office are clamoring for change in the IRS I don't think any significant changed will occur. The IRS is mired in dogma. There will be no significant changes unless the managers who created this monster are removed. The IRS is a survivor. Big brother is out there. Let me introduce you to him.

A Show of Power

About ten o'clock one morning I detected a lot of activity going on around my office. Inasmuch as we had open landscape any significant change in the tempo of activities was easily noticed. I stood up to the full height of my six seven frame and looked around. There were knots of people here and there in serious discussions. About the time I noticed this hubbub the phones in my office began to ring. One of my employees came back to my office and told me there was a big drug bust going down in the Center. I left my office and went out to the central building which was the hub of our five building, twelve acre structure. I though if there was any activity going on it would have to eventually go through this building.

On my way out to the central building I passed groups of employees huddled together. They all seemed distressed. No one was smiling or laughing. They seemed to be afraid. When I arrived in the central building the situation was even worse. Hundreds of people were standing around, dumbfounded looking confused and scared. I had seen this expression a number of times on the faces of people during an earthquake. It is a look of bewildered apprehension and fear. I asked one of the supervisors in the area what had happened. He said a couple of employees had run through the building being chased by some of our Inspectors (IRS cops). No sooner had he said this than a young friend of mine ran through the building. He and I used to play racquetball at one of the local sports clubs. He was a warehouseman and mail person. He had been in my office earlier that morning to drop off some grapes for my staff.

It pained me to see him running for his life like a wild animal. He was some distance from me. He went through so quickly I didn't have a chance to call to him. I wanted to try and calm him down. Tell him there was no escape and ask him to just stand there with me until they came to get him.I stood there in the aisle waiting for the next episode. No one was working in the complex. Six thousand people were milling around in confusion and fear. After about twenty minutes I saw a group of people come into the central building from the warehouse. As they approached I saw that there was one prisoner, my friend flanked by two Inspection agents. He was in handcuffs. They marched him through the central building, through the Administrative building, where my office was located and out to a group of police cars in the front of the building. One by one the six people who were arrested were marched through the gauntlet. I was shocked to see one of my former secretaries. All four foot eleven inches and eighty pounds of her, in handcuffs. The IRS had its show of force. It stopped six thousand people from working to make a point.

We were fortunate that none of the people being chased had a weapon. Innocent people could have been injured or killed if they had a weapon and panicked. Bringing a weapon on the premises would be no more difficult as bringing any kind of contraband in. The IRS could have had these people arrested at home and avoided all of the confusion on the job. It's not like they didn't know where the people lived. The IRS had records of the addresses of the people arrested. The IRS also had plants who had befriended those who were arrested. The plants had attended parties at their homes. There was no way the IRS was going to do the sensible thing and arrest these people at home. The IRS wanted to demonstrate to the masses what big brother would to them if they stepped out of line.

When my friend got out on bail I asked him what happened. He said that a new warehouseman (an IRS plant) had befriended him and asked if he could get him some stuff, (marijuana). The guy asked him to bring it to work. He did what the guy asked him to do. He brought a small amount of POT to work. He offered to give it to the guy but the plant insisted on buying it. My wife and I attended a party one time at my friend's house. I looked back later and remembered seeing the plant at the party. Through a contact in Inspection I found that I was also being watched. Part of the plants report said, "Oscar Williams only drank liquor at the party." What do you call it when someone spies on you in your own home? Here were these inspection plants spying on the suspects and their friends in their homes and writing clandestine reports about people who were not even part of their so-called investigation. Where was their search warrant? What right does the IRS have to spy on citizens in their homes? The IRS's mandate is to collect taxes. There is a name for the IRS's infringement upon some citizens constitutional rights. It's called, "Big brother is watching you."

My former secretary was entrapped just like my racquet-ball buddy. A female plant was put in the Facilities Management Branch as a clerk. She worked her way into the young party crowd and convinced some of them to bring her some pot on the job. They did. They would have given the stuff to her. She insisted on paying them for it. They were charged with possession and selling a controlled substance. The reality is these were just young party people. They certainly weren't pushers or peddlers. I don't believe that they would have brought any marijuana into the office if the two plants had not persuaded them to. This was an obvious case of entrapment. A good lawyer could have certainly beat the rap. They had to depend on public defenders. The IRS had made its point. It had a show of force. Thousands of our employees will always remember the fear, confusion and disruption during the big bust at the Fresno Service Center. This just might dissuade them from getting out of line in the future. Don't want to cross, "Big Brother."

I think it's ironic that after the big bust I saw a branch chief with whom I used to party. The first thing out of my mouth was, "I thought they had you for sure." He came back with the same comment to me. We had a good laugh. Both of us smoked a joint now and then. The real irony of this drug deal is that my branch chief buddy later went into the IRS's Executive Development (XD) program and became a big muck-a-muck in the National Office. He could very well be a director of a service center or district at this time.

As for my friend and former secretary who were marched through the center in shackles and shame, he got a job as a driver for a local company and she got a job as a bank teller.

This show of force is not limited to a show for employees. It is also used against the general public. In the mid eighties a former disgruntled employee began sending me threatening letters. He sent one each month. I had never heard of the man. At that time we had almost six thousand employees. It seems this man took offense at a letter one of my payroll employees had written to him. The letter had told him that the IRS did not owe him the salary he claimed he was owed when he left. I signed the letter. I signed hundreds of letters like that one.

The man's threats became more dramatic. He suggested that the world would be better off without me. I didn't pay too much attention to the letters until he began to attack my race. I knew then that he had found out I was black from an acquaintance or friend who worked at the service center. I became concerned. I talked to the people in our Inspection Office. This is the IRS's police force. They talked to the department of Justice. The Department of Justice said there was nothing they could do unless the man actually tried something. I had no citizens rights because I was a public official.

I was disappointed when I heard this. However, one of the inspectors said, "There is nothing we can do officially, but unofficially we can go out to his house and try and scare him off. The only problem is if we make him angry he could go the other way and try something. Do you want us to try?" I wanted them to try. But I told them not to because I was concerned that he might go the other way and act out his threats. Inspection got me a picture of the man from the Department of Motor vehicles. After about two years the letters stopped. I appreciated the help Inspection offered to give me. The key point here is they were willing to go outside the law to intimidate a civilian to get him to back off. I know I sound like a jerk for ratting on my inspection buddies who were trying to help me but, this kind of thing is what makes some citizens fear the

Government and the black helicopter coming in at night to reap some kind of unofficial justice.

The, "kick my dog you kick me," syndrom is a part of the IRS's mentality. Here is an example of that mind set. This was an article which ran in the Fresno Bee in June 1997:

JUDGE REPRIMANDS IRS FOR ABUSING AUTHORITY
Fresno Bee June 6, 1997

Woman awarded $325,000 after claiming Retaliation by agent.

DENVER—In hindsight, insulting the IRS agent during an audit was probably not a good idea. But Carole Ward let fly with this gem: "Honey, from what I can see of your accounting skills, the country would be better served if you were dishing up chicken-fried steak on some interstate in west Texas, with all the clunky jewelry and big hair." A short time later, federal agents raided her son's business and then released confidential information about her taxes to the media in what Ward called "character assassination."

This week, a federal judge reprimanded the IRS for its actions and awarded the woman about $325,000 in damages and attorneys fees. "By this award, this court gives notice to the IRS that reprehensible abuse of authority by one of its employees cannot and will not be tolerated." U.S. district Judge William Downes said after the non-jury trial, "Part of the responsibility requires that you accept criticism, however inaccurate and/or unjustified in silence." Ward, 49, said she is not proud of what she said to auditor Paula Dzieranoewski during the 1993 audit. The meeting was one of several regarding income taxes owed by the children's clothing stores owned by her son, Tristan, then 20.

Two weeks later, IRS agents seized and padlocked the stores with a so-called jeopardy assessment demanding $325,000 in back taxes from Ward. "Such an order is considered extreme and is normally used when the IRS fears it is in danger of never collecting the taxes," said Ward's attorney, William C. Walker. "Wards family depended on the stores as their sole source of income, and the seizer put them in desperate straits."

In order for the IRS to do the degree of damage it did to this family every level of management had to sanction the illegal actions. The sad part of this is the fine of $325,000 did not come out of the pocket of one of the IRS participants. The fine was paid by the taxpayers. You would think that anyone involved in these blatant get even tactics would have been fired. However, that is not the case. All of them continue drawing their salaries as if nothing happened. Even though the agency was publicly humiliated by the judge and the press the people involved go unscathed. There is no question in my mind that privately they say, "We taught that big mouthed women a lesson. The next big mouth person won't open their mouth so fast." When there is no individual or organizational accountability the IRS its managers can do anything they chose to do.

Earlier in this chapter I mentioned how the IRS not only intimidates outsiders but it will also turn on its own. This mentality says, "If you are not with us, then you must be against us." The following article appeared in the Fresno Bee in April of 1999:

Job threat against IRS agent assailed

Houston officials are
suspected of retaliating
for woman's testimony.

Fresno Bee April 17, 1999

WASHINGTON—A star (IRS) witness at 1997 senate hearings into tax payers abuse by the Internal Revenue Service said Friday that her managers moved to fire her but quickly retreated after the agencies top brass and the Senate learned of the action.

Jennifer Long, a Houston IRS agent, said she was called in from an audit Thursday–the tax filing deadline for millions if Americans–and told she would be fired in 60 days if her job performance did not improve. Asked if she considered the firing threat to be retribution for her Senate testimony, Long said, "there is no question about it." Senate Finance Committee Chairman William V. Roth Jr., who conducted two sets of hearings on IRS abuse, and IRS Commissioner Charles O. Rossotti said they would begin investigations immediately.

The thirteen page letter notifying Long of "ongoing performance deficiencies" was withdrawn Friday by Houston officials, she said. At least one official subsequently was placed on administrative leave, sources said.

Long, a 16-year IRS agent, testified that IRS managers fabricated evidence to show that taxpayers owed more taxes than they reported and that they targeted low-income people who do not have the resources to fight back.

Before her testimony, Long received "fully successful" job ratings, but her ratings dropped to failing after her testimony, the finance Committee said. In Thursday' notice warning of possible dismissal, IRS manager Karie L. Gulley criticized

how Long planned and scheduled her work and the time she
spent preparing for taxpayer audits.

Long said her managers continually harassed her because
she dares to criticize the agency. Last week, she said, "they were
livid, they got really mad," when the IRS learned she had given
an interview to ABC's "20/20" news program.

Roth called the warning notice sent to Long a, "clear act
of retaliation. The actions of the IRS management in the
Houston office are outrageous."

Rosetti said he was, "extemely disturbed that we may have
taken an action that could be retaliatory." He reiterated
previous statements that he, will not tolerate retaliation against
employees who testify or report wrong doing.

The Senate hearings concerning the egregious acts by the
IRS were carried out in 1997 and 1998. The outcome of
these hearing resulted in one thing, an oversight committee
to oversee the IRS. The oversight committee can over see
forever, but the rotten apples, the IRS mangers who led the
agency in the atrocities are still in the barrel. Their attitude
is frozen in time. Nothing is going to change the prevailing
attitude of intimidation, cover up and save my ass. The only
thing which will ever get this agency to function properly
within our democracy is to dump all of the rotten apples
out of the IRS management barrel and staff the agency
with proven managers from other Government offices or
from private industry. There is no chance of this ever
happening. There no chance the IRS managers will change
their modes operandi.

Pecking Order

My first introduction to the status symbols or pecking order system within the IRS began when I received my name plate. This is a little thing but it focused my attention on how the IRS protects its tier system of importance. The name plate I received looked like it came from the Mickey Mouse section of some five and dime store. I called the section chief whose people made the name plates. I said to him, "I hope my name plate didn't cause some kind of material shortage."After he stopped laughing, he explained that name plate size was based upon a persons position. I was given a standard branch chiefs name plate. In twenty years of Government service I had never heard of anything so silly.

I had not requested a name plate because I brought my nameplate with me. It was cast iron, with a raised border and lettering, with a dull black background. It was ten inches long and over two inches tall. The little piece of junk the IRS gave me was about one inch in height and six inches long. My name was embossed on a strip of some type of plastic. I tossed the IRS's in the trash. As my tenure continued I began to observe name plates throughout the various offices. I could see why almost everyone who came into my office mentioned how attractive my name plate was. The size and quality of material made me an equal to the regional commissioner.

We also had status furniture. Like the name plate I think the furniture was provided to help managers remember what level they were within the organization. Maybe it was designed to help the managers know who they were. If a

manager should forget who he was he could just take a
look at his nameplate and furnishings and guess what level
of management he represented. Division chiefs had a two
piece combo. There was a three partitioned section about
seven feet tall. The partitions were hinged together so that
the two outer sections could be angled in order to stand
up. The center portion had a little shelf which served as a
desk. The two side sections had a box type of filing
container attached to them. They also had about a four foot
diameter round coffee table. We branch chief types had a
cheaper four piece combo which consisted of three filing
cabinets six feet by four feet, and a round table which was
about four feet in diameter and stood three feet tall. I never
did figure out what good it was. It was too tall to be considered a coffee table and to small to hold anything. After
staring at that thing for a few years sitting in various places
in my office I had The Facilities management Branch take
it away. Section chiefs had a cheaper combo and lower level
supervisors had desk. One afternoon I got a call from the
chief of the Personnel Branch. He invited me to come to
his office and see his new furniture. When I walked into
his office I immediately saw that he had a division chief's
combo. I congratulated him on his good fortune in getting
a promotion. He grinned like the old fox he was and said,
"I didn't get promoted. The Facilities Branch had one set
left over. Being the tenured branch chief in the organization, they gave it to me."

The following morning a buddy of mine came into my
office with the latest gossip. The hot question of the
moment was, "did I hear what had happened to the
Personnel Branch chief's furniture."

My response was, "Of course I know. He got a division chief combo yesterday."

He said, "you better go down and take a look."He refused to tell me what was going on. I went down to the Personnel Branch Chief'S office and stopped dumbfounded. The division chief combo was gone. His old furniture was back in place. The branch chief was sitting in a chair with his feet on the desk and his chin on his chest. I could see he was not a happy camper.

I asked, "What happened to your new furniture?"

He raised his head, looked at me and said, "Bob, (our division chief) had it removed overnight."

I asked, "Did he say anything to you about this?"

He said, "No. I came in this morning and here was my old furniture."

I was not surprised because this is the kind of petty thing I expected from Bob. Bob put the Personnel Branch chief in his place, without saying one word. I think Bob should have got the jerk of the century award for pulling this dirty trick.

Make Me a Star

I found the IRS's management training programs were as bogus as their convoluted names. I had been in the IRS about two years when my boss suggested that I apply for the Regional Management Careers Program (RMCP). This is a program for up and comers. Those in the programs received a few perks. The primary perk was occasional developmental assignments. The other perk was people in the program were automatically considered for some positions without having to apply for them. I really wasn't interested but since my boss suggested I apply I decided to play the game. I submitted my application. A few weeks later he called and told me that I had not been accepted into the program. He told me not to be discouraged because most people don't make it the first time. I wasn't crushed but I was curious to know why I was rejected. He said that he didn't know, but he had asked the Assistant Regional commissioner for Human resources, to fly down from San Francisco and critique me. His name is Wassenaur. For simplicity lets just call him, "Muck."

Late the next week I got a call from my chief. He told me Muck would be in soon. After Muck arrived, I went over to my division chiefs office to meet with him. It was just the three of us. My chief, the Muck and me. We talked about the weather and finally got around to talking about the program. I told muck I had a question about the program. I said, "In the Regional statement of our mission, it says that we will make an assessment of (mission) results. I would like to see an assessment of the effectiveness of the RMCP." I had asked my division chief this same question a short time ago. He said he didn't know of any type of assessment of the program. He suggested I ask Muck when he came down. Furrows appeared in Mucks forehead. He said, "The program has proven itself." I responded, "This may be true but I would still like to see some type of analysis. This is an old program and keeping with our Regional mission statement, someone must have take a critical look at this program." Muck looked across the coffee table at me for a long moment. I think this is what is called composing ones self. He finally replied, "To my knowledge there is no data. There is no data or analysis because a program like this does not require an assessment." I didn't pursue the issue any further. I could see he was getting upset.

He said, "I came down to talk to you because I thought it would be better if we spoke face to face rather than on the phone." I thanked him for that consideration. He continued, "The primary reason you were not accepted into the program is because every time your name comes up in the hallway or the bathroom someone always has something negative to say about you."

I had to mentally shake my head to be sure I had heard what the Muck had said. I had been reclining in my chair with my foot on my chiefs coffee table. I straightened up, leaned as far as I could across the coffee table, looked Muck in the eye and said, "You are telling me you flew all the way down here to tell me I was rejected for the program because of shithouse rumors." I have never been accused of having a lot of tact. Muck said, "You're taking my words out of context. What I meant was that in informal situations when your name comes up no one has anything positive to say about you." I asked, "Is this supposed to be some kind of popularity contest. I wasted my damn time filling out all of those papers and they mean nothing because it all comes down to shithouse rumors." The muck lost his cool. "Okay." he snarled. "If you want a report on Oscar Williams, I'm going to get you one." He got up and stomped out of the office. My division chief and I sat there for a moment. He said, "I don't think he likes you." we both had a good laugh at that.

This was my first division chief, Harvey Kuffner. I worked for three different division chiefs. Harvey was the one I was closes to and respected the most. I guess I felt this way because he was a lot like me. He didn't fit into the IRS system. He had yelling matches with the assistant director which could be heard for a hundred yards away. I think he tried to do what was right rather than what was politically correct. I don't know how he ever got to be a division chief in the environment we existed in. I have to give him credit he was smart enough to get out. He gave up his division chief position, accepted the job as the night manager, went back to college to change his career. He left the IRS and started a successful computer consulting business. My second division chief was Bob Maddux. Basically I felt nothing but contempt for bob. As I mentioned earlier I thought he had a huge ego and little substance. My third and last division chief was Glen Coles. I liked Glen. At times I could see our relationship was tempered by the fact Glen was a company man. In spite of that I respected him as a person.

Back to Muck and his trip back to San Francisco to get a report on Oscar Williams. After Muck returned to the Region, I got a phone call from the chief of the Budget Section, Joe Mc Clendon. He asked me what in the world I did to muck to make him so angry? He said Muck called a special meeting of all of his office heads. In this meeting he directed each office head to give him a written report about Oscar Williams. I told him what had happened between Muck and me. By the time I had finished my story he was almost hysterical with laughter.

When he finally stopped laughing, he said he had to give Muck a report on me. He said he would send me a copy of his report. He said, "My people and I don't have any problems with you or your staff. I don't know what this guy is looking for. I'll send the copy of the report in a confidential envelope. Use it any way you have to." I thanked him for his support. I didn't get any calls from any of the other office heads. The Budget Section Chief was like my first division chief. He marched to his own tune. He also left the IRS and built a lucrative accounting business. It seems sort of odd but over the years all of the people I established a close relationship with left the IRS. I often look back and wonder if I should have followed their example.

I received the copy of the report about me. The weeks went by. Once in a while my boss would ask if I had heard anything from Muck. I told him not a word. Finally he said he was going to call Muck. After all, Muck had promised to get this report and get back with us. He called. Muck said he would hop a plane and come down. He came down in a couple of days. When he arrived I went over to my bosses office. There we were again, grouped around the little round coffee table. He got right to the point. He looked me in the eye and said, "I thought about what I told you I was going to do. After thinking about it, I decided it was not the thing to do. If I asked my people for a report on you, they might think I was out to get Oscar. I didn't want to convey that feeling to my staff."

I sat there speechless, dumbfounded. I just sat there looking at him. I started to say, "You are a God damn liar. I have a copy of one of the reports." It took all of the effort I could muster to say nothing. My acquaintance told me to use the report as I saw fit. I interpreted him to mean if I was threatened in some way. Muck was certainly no threat. In my opinion he was just blatantly dishonest, deceitful and stupid. I didn't see any threat in this so I didn't tell Muck he was a liar because I had a copy of one of the reports he requested. I just sat there and stared at him in disbelief. He went on to say, "It seems we got off to a bad start. This has not been a good experience for either of us. The regional Management Careers Program is a good program. I have thought about your candidacy. I suggest you apply next year. My speech returned. I thanked him and left the office before I said something I might regret.

Later Harvey, my boss called me and asked me what was wrong. He said, "You let him off the hook. That's not like you." I told him about the phone call from the budget section chief and about the copy of the report which he sent to me. My chief was shocked. He said he was sincerely sorry for the charade Muck had pulled on me. He apologized for what had happened, because he felt responsible for what had occurred because he encouraged me to put in for the program. I assured him it was no big deal. I was a big boy and could deal with it.

I did not apply for the program again. I felt that if Muck was an example of the product I didn't want any part of it. Just out of curiosity before I retired I looked up Muck in the National Office phone directory. I saw that he had become a bigger MUCK in IRS's National Office in Washington D.C.

(XD) Extra Dumb

The IRS has another management development program called the Executive Development (XD) program. This is a national program which is alleged to prepare managers for positions such as assistant directors and assistant regional commissioners. I mentioned my encounter with one of these new shave tail assistant directors in the first chapter of this book when we had major payroll problems. He is the one I asked to butt out of my business.

Usually about six people are selected for this program during each of its cycles. They are taken off of their regular jobs and spend about two years carousing around the U. S. being developed. Over the years I have given my financial dog and pony show (show and tell) to the groups when they filtered through the Fresno Service Center. I realized that I should start thinking about retirement when there were three of my old drinking and pot smoking cronies in the last three groups which came through the center.

I had not seen any of them for about five years. Each of them dropped in to say hello before the dog and pony show. All of them declined my invitation to go to the old watering hole, the Checkmate to reminiscent over old times. I realize now that because they were in line to become a biggie they couldn't be seen fraternizing with the likes of me, the black sheep of the organization. They reminded me of Mormon missionaries. They stayed together, ate together and except for their gender they even looked like one another.

The program is very expensive. The candidates are being paid at the GS-15 level, about eighty-five thousand a year. With benefits this comes to about one hundred thousand a year for each candidate. The group is on the road for almost two years. This entails a large chunk of travel funds. This cost about forty-five thousand a year per person. The bottom line is that it cost about one and a half million dollars to develop a group of these people.

Back when I was a candidate for the Regional Management Careers Program (RMCP), remember Mucks program, I asked to see some type of comparative data assessing the effectiveness of the program. There was none. When I heard about the XD program out of curiosity, I asked to see some form of evaluation or assessment of the program, i.e., some kind of data where someone had compared the effectiveness of the managers who completed this program against those in other agencies who had not been part of a similar program. There was none. One of the most hilarious subjective assessments of the program came from, of all places, a congressman. During a budget hearing out of the clear blue sky he lauded the Executive Development program of the IRS. I can just see this congressman sitting there at a free lunch, sponsored by some IRS official being pumped full of hot air about the XD program. He goes back to the IRS appropriation hearings and belches out, "Give them the money, they have a great XD program." What do you expect from a congressman?

If this program is so great why did President Clinton call for a clean sweep of the IRS managers in 1997? He said, 'Get rid of the bean counters and replace them with managers." When thinking about the effectiveness of the IRS's, XD program consider the following:

AROUND WASHINGTON   Fresno Bee June 25, 1997
Board created to improve IRS

President Bill Clinton has created a new board to help
the Treasury Department improve its management of the
troubled Internal Revenue Service.

The president signed an executive order creating the
Internal Revenue Service Board. The panel of administration
officials will focus on management, operational and customer
service issues. The move is part of a broader effort by the
Treasury Department to implement a plan to improve the tax-
collecting agency. The IRS has come under fire for a litany
of problems, from failing to upgrade its computers to shoddy
customer service.

Even the Congress is getting smart or they are just
getting on the band wagon. The following newspaper
article shows their concern with the current management
system of the IRS:

San Francisco Examiner April 13, 1997
A COMMISSION,
GRIM AND GRUMBLING, AUDITS THE IRS

Washington. While most of us scramble to finish our tax
returns, two of the more independent and capable members
of Congress are putting the finishing touches on a report
which conceivably could make future dealings with the
Internal Revenue Service less of an ordeal. Sen. Bob Kerry,
D-Neb., and Rep. Rob Portman, R-Ohio, actually have a
chance to do something good for the taxpayers of this country.

They are the co-chairman of the bipartisan National
Commission on Restructuring the Internal Revenue Service,

created last year by Congress and due to submit its final report by the end of June.

The horror stories about the IRS have become so widely publicized that few can dispute that this is a bureaucracy in big trouble.

Fresno Bee 2/1/97

IRS REORGANIZATION IS URGED
AMID COMPUTER MODERNIZATION FIASCO

WASHINGTON—The most sweeping reorganization of the IRS since 1952 when it was a patronage agency riddled with corruption, was proposed Friday by the co-chairman of the bipartisan panel investigating the agencies bungled effort to modernize its computers.

The co-chairman, Sen. Bob Kerrey, D-Neb., and Rep. Rob Portman, R-Ohio, said that a board of directors should be installed to oversee the IRS and that the agencies next commissioner should have a strong management background or should be a senior aide with experience.

Fresno Bee 2/8/97

IRS WANTS $500m FOR COMPUTERS

WASHINGTON—The Internal Revenue Service is seeking $500 million to modernize its troubled computer system as it tries to recover from a widely criticized push to update its computers. Deputy Treasury Secretary Lawrence Summers, who is overseeing the IRS modernization and reforms, hinted Friday that the agencies computer woes may not be over. He declined to elaborate. So far, the IRS has canceled $1 billion in contracts covering 26 programs from the earlier modernization effort.

Wall Street Journal August 1999
IRS Says Fixing Internal Problems May Take Years

WASHINGTON—Some solutions to the Internal Revenue Services financial-management problems may take years to put in place, the agency said.

This assessment came in the IRS's response to a General Accounting Office report which says the agency continues to suffer from a broad range of internal weaknesses. The GAO report released this week, said these weaknesses have resulted in disbursement of fraudulent and other questionable tax refunds, unnecessary burdens to taxpayers resulting from taxpayer receipts stolen by IRS employees, and errors and delays in posting payments to taxpayersaccounts. The Congressional watchdog agency said IRS control weaknesses fall into five areas: failing to track unpaid assessments; security over taxpayer receipts and taxpayer information; providing improper refunds and earned-income tax credits; failing to report revenue and distribution; and poor untimely financial reporting. The GAO said some of these weaknesses are long standing, but added we have found that some weaknesses are more pervasive thanpreviously reported. The Congressional agency said it has found weaknesses regarding the security of receipts and taxpayer information in varying degrees at all ten IRS service centers, at other IRS offices and at banks that process taxpayer receipts for the IRS. In the area of security over receipts and taxpayer information, the GAO said the IRS's internal controls don't adequately safeguard assets such as cash, checks and sensitive taxpayer information from loss or theft. At four IRS service centers, the GAO said background check results disclosed that 273, or 5.1% , of 5400 employees hired to handle taxpayerdata and/or receipts had falsified information on their applications and that 64, or 23%, of these 273 persons had significant unsuitable backgrounds, such as criminal convictions, which resulted in their termination or forced resignation.

Ben Wenzel, a deputy IRS commissioner, stressed in commenting on the report that even as the IRS works to implement some recommended short-term changes, "some of the solutions while–while ultimately achievable–may take years to put in place." Elsewhere in his comment letter, the IRS official said, "Often, seemingly straightforward steps to solve problems are much more complicated than would first appear."

(End of newspaper articles)

I could go on endlessly citing congressional hearings; GAO reports; and IRS atrocities affecting taxpayers. However, appalling is the only word which describes the dismal state which the IRS management system has created. I think President Clinton gave them far to much credit when he called them, "Bean Counters." They can't even count beans!

The questions which must and should be answered is, "Why has the IRS failed in so many areas if their vaunted expensive (XD) Executive development program is so great? Where were all of these highly paid IRS Executive Development (XD) graduates when the organization was going down the drain?" The preceding newspaper articles detailing the loss of hundreds of millions of taxpayers dollars, an antiquated financial accounting system and an unresponsive management system speaks for itself. This gives an objective evaluation of the IRS's failed Executive Development (XD) program.

The concern of The Congress and the president concerning the IRS's inept management practices provides another assessment of the Executive Development program. If the IRS was a private enterprise all of the top executives and managers would be removed from their jobs. Based upon my experiences with the IRS I would bet my last dollar that years from now you will see the same faces in the IRS hierarchy. They have a way of surviving. After all of the Congressional hearings, GAO reports and airing of the IRS's dirty laundry you would think that some intelligent person in the White House or the Congress would say, "Junk that IRS Executive Development Program which spawned the executives who created the mess the IRS is in." To date no one has said one word. The program continues to go on turning out more inept, incompetent and rich IRS executives, who make excuses for their ineptness.

Someone to Watch over Them

The National Treasury Employee Union (NTEU) has historically had a social agenda. They sponsored sports activities, fund raisers etc. This began to change as the distance between the haves, IRS managers and the have nots, IRS workers widened. In addition to this there was a management void just asking to be filled. The rank and file were not privy to inflated grades, fat awards and the outrageous bonuses of the Senior Executive Service managers.After a number of years playing the social gadfly the NTEU began getting away from the parties and started some serious negotiations with the IRS. One of the first things they tried to sell the IRS on was the production incentive pay system. They pushed for the use of average standards to set incentive pay thresholds at which point incentive pay begins.

When I heard what the union was pushing for I looked up our management negotiator and suggested to him that the IRS insist on using engineered standards to set incentive pay. He gave me the usual IRS managers blank star. I tried to explain to him that engineered standards are set by predetermined time systems such as Methods Time Measurement or time study. They were much more exacting and less flexible than average standards. I had used a number of these techniques when I was in industrial engineering in other agencies to set production standards. When I finished my explanation the IRS negotiator gave me the same blank stare I have seen so often on the faces of IRS managers.

I gave up. The difference in standards may seem trivial but the difference between engineered standards, which I would have pushed for and the average standards the union wanted could equate to hundreds of thousands of dollars a year. The IRS bought the union's proposal–hook, line and sinker. I guess there is some form of righteousness in this. Like management the employees on the bottom of the ladder now had their bloated awards system. Any normal employee could exceed the average standard with little effort. After the incentive pay system was implemented many employees, incentive pay exceeded the amount of their normal salary.

Each year when the union contract came up for negotiations I watched with amusement the hunkering down of the IRS managers. The union always went into the negotiations with less and came out with more. I was fascinated watching the rank and file people out negotiate the high paid IRS management teams. One time just before negotiations started, I made a facetious comment to one of our management negotiators. I suggested that the IRS could save a lot of time if it made up a list before hand of what it was going to give up. At the beginning of the negotiation the IRS could give the list to the union and ask what do you want next year? He didn't take my comment in the spirt it was given. Then again, considering how pissed off he was at my suggestion, maybe he did take it in the right spirt.

The union also became a watch dog of the IRS management system. For example the Fresno Bee ran an article on May 17, 1985 which said, "50,000 protest letters destroyed by the IRS." The article went on to say, "The National Treasury Employees Union, Local 97 said the letters were destroyed from January through March (1985) to alleviate a heavy work backlog and to help managers with merit pay by increasing production." The IRS denied it. The union went to the press with the same charges concerning the Austin, Service Center. Finally the IRS commissioner, Roscoe L Egger Jr. confirmed there had been some mistakes made. Roscoe held no one responsible for the, so called, mistakes. In fact it is a matter of record that during the two years 1985 and 1986 when these mistakes occurred the directors of the Fresno and Austin Service Centers received Senior Executive bonuses of about $10,000 each.

For some years the IRS has been trying to downsize. The key to their plan was to lop off a lot of little guys at the bottom of the rung while protecting their good old boys at the top. This would place hundreds of little people on the unemployment line. During this process they kept moving their good old boys around to protect them. My old Fiscal Officer position is a good example of the games they were playing. After I left the IRS my assistant competed for and was promoted into my old position. When the downsizing started the IRS put one of their regional good old boys into my old position at a GS-13 level. This is one grade higher than my old grade. My former assistant still kept her promotion to a GS-12 but she was no longer called the Fiscal Officer. I saw the good old boy at a going away party and I mentioned to him I had heard he had my old job. He replied, "I don't know anything about fiscal, Lois (my ex-assistant) still runs the office. Finally he was placed somewhere else. They had a need to place another good old boy. He was a GS-14. No problem—just raise my old job, two grades to a GS-14. Change the title to Comptroller and stick the good old boy in there. The IRS is also offering a number of employees a fat severance package to entice them to retire. This has been in the range of twenty to thirty thousand dollars. This is going to end up costing the taxpayers millions of dollars. All of this could have been avoided if the IRS had simply declared a reduction in force. This would have saved the taxpayers the millions of dollars which are now being wasted because of bureaucratic fumbling in the dark.

There are two drawbacks to a reduction in force. One is under a reduction in force. The IRS cannot just move their good old boys around at will to protect them. There are Civil Service rules which must be followed which limit geographic placement and establishes what are called bumping rights. The second problem is the IRS has again negotiated away their position with the union and are now in catch 22. The article below shows how the union was holding IRS's feet to the fire:

Fresno Bee 3/24/97

IRS DEADLINE TODAY ON LAYOFF POLICY

WASHINGTON—The IRS is struggling to meet a deadline today on key labor issues–how to handle layoffs of hundreds of workers. Despite months of negotiations, the agency and the workers union still disagree on basic issues. The Internal Revenue Service and the National Treasury Employees Union–which represents 90,000 IRS workers–must reach agreement on the layoffs today or turn the dispute over to the Federal Services Impasses Panel.

The glaring issue is not the growing strength of the union. The real problem is the IRS managers have abandoned their responsibilities. Over the years the union through negotiation and every day consultations have filled the void left by management. Basically the union is micro managing the IRS. President Clinton should consider the union people as replacements for the, "Bean Counters," he wants to replace. I think they would excel in running the organization just as they have excelled and prevailed in the negotiations and consultations with IRS managers.

Studies in Frustration

One of the responsibilities of my office was to do management analysis studies. These types of studies used scientific approaches to study management and administrative systems. We used various techniques such as random sampling; statistical analysis; regression analysis; time study; work station analysis; work flow analysis; time study; and Methods time Measurement (M.M.). I had one management analyst on my staff. In addition to the one analyst I always had employees assigned to my office for developmental training. I usually cross trained them as management analyst and budget analyst.

I had performed these types of studies for years, when I worked for the Department of Defense (DOD). My studies were used by the managers in DOD to measure the efficiency of their organization; eliminate unnecessary task; simplify work flow; and in some instances these things led to a reduction in personnel. However, I was baffled when I did studies for the IRS and the managers gave them a cursory look and stuck them in a file to rot. Finally the light began to dawn when I realized what the problem was. I began to realize that many of the early studies performed by my office were not utilized by IRS managers because they lacked the necessary knowledge on how to use them.President Clinton was correct in his analysis of IRS managers, when he said, "IRS managers are bean counters." I began to see this truth. They weren't managers. They were highly paid bean counters who had worked their way up the ranks, into a management position with no formal or informal training in the scientific forms of management.

A study we did which illustrates the problem was done by a female supervisor who was assigned to my office from the operating area for developmental training. As part of her training I assigned her the task of doing a productivity study of all of the Human Resources division branches. I guided her through each step in the process. She did an excellent job. When the study was completed we gave a copy of the report to each branch manager. The IRS managers looked at the study, gave it a cursory nod of their heads and stuck it in a file. The Personnel Branch did change the physical layout of their office to conform to our suggested layout to better serve their customers.

That was it. Out of four studies totaling about one hundred and twenty pages of data and suggestions, the physical layout of one office was changed.

In previous offices I had worked in before going to the IRS, the managers would have used this study to re-engineer the duties of some positions to increase efficiency, improve the work flow and eliminate unnecessary functions. This sometimes resulted in a reduction in staffing, but this was not the prime purpose of the study. They would have used the work measurement elements on an on going basis to continually monitor the effectiveness of their organization. The IRS managers had no clue. I might be as well had given them forty blank pages.

The irony of this is that the woman who was detailed to my office got a promotion to the Regional office as a Program Analyst. She went back to night school to get her masters degree. She called and asked me if it would be okay to use the study she had done as a basis for her masters degree. I assured her it was fine with me, and wished her luck. She eventually got her masters degree. It turned out the study was not a complete lost.

Another study my office performed early in our tenure was the study of seasonal salaries. They fluctuated so much doing the season it was difficult to get a fix on them at any particular time. An error in projecting these salaries could result in significant erroneous dollar variances in projecting salaries. Most offices used the guess and by golly system or the wild-ass-guess (WAG) when projecting seasonal salary requirements.

In an attempt to get us out of the green eye shade and rolled up cuff era, my staff developed a system of projecting salaries utilizing regression analysis. This was before computers back in the early seventies. Along with the study we developed a program to run the projection on a programable calculator. This was the predecessor of the computer. We sent copies of the study and the program to the Regional office and all other offices which had Fiscal Officers. I didn't hear one blip from the other offices. Nothing. I called a couple of offices to be sure they received our material. They had, but hadn't had enough time to look at it. Later I realized that my office was probably one of the few offices which had a programable calculator. The program would have been of no value to them. However, the regression analysis application was valid and my staff could have taught other people to use them. No one asked. The end of another study in frustration.

I was getting desperate in my attempt to find some area to perform studies which IRS managers and supervisors might be able to comprehend. I decided to do a study of our security system. Security was becoming more of a concern within the IRS. I don't know if it was paranoia or the surfacing of so many radical anti-tax groups.

The security system consisted of various electrical and physical security systems throughout our twelve-acre complex, under roof plus the parking lots. Because of the size of the study I worked with my analyst quite a bit on this project. I had some fun on this project. One day I was studying the magnetic switches on the emergency exit doors. There were number of doors throughout the center. They were not locked, but they could not be opened from the outside. If a door was opened from the inside it set off an alarm and it showed the location of the open door on the security council. After an alarm sounded guards were immediately dispatched to the door. Many of theses doors were secluded and in darkened areas of the building at night.

I had my analyst get some clear tape and a screw driver. I wrapped the tape around the two halves of the magnetic switch on one door. I unscrewed the screws which held half of the switch to the door. I then pushed the door open. My analyst yelled, "Don't do that it will set off the alarms." The door swung open. Nothing happened. I explained to my analyst that because the two halves of the magnetic switch were still together, the magnetic circuit was not broken and the switch thinks the door is still closed. I pointed out to him that the switches should have been installed with one way screws, which cannot be unscrewed. We put everything back. Later after we had completed the study we did a demonstration for the security chief. Our study pointed out that an inside person could by pass the switches like we did, on all of the doors throughout the center allowing intruders to enter the center after dark to plant explosives, take hostages or steal equipment.

In the fields of analysis and auditing it is common courtesy to give a draft to the responsible offices before preparing a final report. Most of the responsibility for security was in the Human Resources division. I gave the chief, who was also my boss, a draft copy of our report. When he saw one of the items in the study he blanched. I am a pilot. I own a Cessna 172. That is probably why I thought of a possible attack on the center by air. I simply pointed out in the study that a terrorist could fly his small plane over the center and level the center with a few pieces of dynamite. He called me over to his office to discuss this item. He was visibly upset. He wanted me to exclude this portion of the study. All that I suggested was that we train our employees to take cover under their desk if explosions begin occurring. This could save people from falling debris and from being trampled as everyone ran for the exits.

In California we were taught to get under our desk from the time we were in kindergarten in case of an earthquake. Within the center we trained our people not to pick up suspicious objects because it could be an explosive. We ran mock test by planting suspicious packages in various areas. One day I was standing in front of a urinal in the bathroom. Standing like this some time the eyes wander around. There on the floor was a round cylinder about eight inches long. My heart skipped a beat before I realized it was a plant. I dutifully washed my hands, went to my office and reported the object to security. They were proud of me. I argued with my chief to keep my idea of training employees in case of an air attack in the study. I pointed out to him that the mock bomb planting test and the fire drills we had were training exercises no different from what I recommended. He still insisted that I take all references to an air attack upon the center out of the study. I took it out. I can only assume that deep down inside he feared that someone might see the study and try to act it out.

It is ironic that in the early nineties, shortly after I had retired a disgruntled engineer from southern California, launched a couple of home made grenades into the Fresno Service Center's parking lot, with his home made grenade launcher. He was apprehended before he did any real damage. They were lucky he wasn't a pilot.

The report was finally published. After all parties had time to study the report my chief, the Chief of the Human Resources division and I sat down and went through it item by item. In essence we went through the study and he told me which portions of the study would be incorporated and which portions would not. To some degree I was perturbed by some of the negative input. On the other hand I felt a sense of relief, because for the first time IRS managers read and understood a study which my office had produced. I had succeeded in dumbing down my studies to the point where even an IRS manager could understand it. I felt good. I had succeeded against insurmountable ignorance.

Bye the way, the screws were replaced on the magnetic switches on the emergency doors with one way screws.

Another item our study pointed out was that the only outside air intake for the complete complex was next to one of the parking lots. It was open and totally unprotected. This left the facility vulnerable to anyone who chose to walk by and toss a cannister of nerve gas or another type of gas into the intake vent. This would disrupt the total organization and dependent upon the material could result in personnel injury. We recommended building a containment with a locked door around the inlet. Management disagreed with this because they thought the possibility of this happening was very remote. I argued that the guards at all entrances looked in all packages to ensure that dangerous material was not brought into the center. I pointed out that if someone wanted to do some type of harm to the center they could bypass the entrances and simply sabotage the air system. I argued that the unguarded air system was just another unguarded entrance into the center. My argument fell upon deaf ears.

The purpose of a security system is for the protection of life, limb and property. My analyst and I found that during the winter months, the intake of outside air was reduced to cut down on heating cost. We noted in our study that during the flu season November through march the sick leave rate soared. We recommended that the following year a test be run by bringing in more fresh air. We would compare the sick leave records with the previous seasons and see if there was a significant reduction. Salaries are the most expensive thing we pay for. We contended that because of reduced sick leave and increased production there might be a net savings of money. More important we pointed out our employees would suffer less from airborne illnesses.

Of course there was no test made. We continued making our employees sick by circulating stagnant germ laden air in the winter. Again irony raises its little head. Years after our study was done the Federal Aeronautics Administration (FAA) made the airlines begin to increase the amount of outside air in there airliners. Just like the IRS, over the years the airlines had been reducing the amount of outside air to reduce the cost of fuel needed to heat the outside air before it was sent into the cabin. The FAA'S order to the airlines came about because they had noted an increase in passenger illness because of airborne infections caused by the circulation of stagnant contaminated air. Is the FAA inherently more intelligent than IRS managers in recognizing the problem associated with stagnant air and airborne illnesses? Or does the FAA care more about the health of passengers than the IRS cares for its employees? I think the answer to both questions is yes.

Another item in the study was rejected because rank has its privilege. We knew that all packages and briefcases brought into the center had to be opened and inspected by the guards at the entrances. During the study we found that the director's staff brought their briefcases or packages into the center without being inspected. It has been established long ago in the military that a security system which had exceptions was as good as no security system at all. We took this position in our study and recommended that all packages and briefcases be inspected at the entrances. It did not take a lot of imagination to see that a radical person or group could note this exception to the security system. They could take hostage a family of the director's staff and force the IRS manager to carry explosives into the center. The Chief of the Human Resources Division would not even discuss this with the director. This idea of terrorist groups attacking the IRS may seem extreme. But a few years after our study was done a group of survivalist separatist were foiled in an attempt to bomb the Ogden Utah Service Center VIA the mail. What do you think they would have done in Fresno if they knew of the hole in our security?

One of the best things I ever did for myself and the organization was to eliminate the position of management analyst when the position became vacant. I also eliminated training in this area of people who were detailed to my office for development. By doing this I eliminated my frustration and that of the IRS managers who no longer had to look at the studies from my office and wonder what language they were written in.

Ask and Yee May Receive

Sometimes people ask for things which they really don't want. In one of his weekly show and tell meetings with his staff, (His division chiefs) the director told them to solicit suggestions from their people on ways to improve the efficiency of the center. Inasmuch as my office's job was to analyze and make recommendations for improving efficiency in December of 1979 I wrote a report in response to the directors request.

I wrote a critique on each level of management. I detailed the problems which deterred from its efficient operation and made suggestions as to improving its effectiveness. For eight years I had watched our stumbling bumbling managers making the same mistakes over and over and no one asked, "What is wrong with our management system?" I had been collecting data on these problems over the years. I didn't know what I was going to do with the data, but I felt compelled to collect it; analyze it; and store it away. I realized that the director wanted the usual mundane suggestions on improving production. However, he didn't specify production in his request for efficiency improvement suggestions and I wasted no time in preparing my report and submitting it to my division chief, Bob. The report dealt primarily with problem resolution at the level of the director, division and branch chiefs. These are the levels of management which are involved in the decision making process within the center.

In general the report provides examples of how management continued to make the same mistakes repeatedly. Managers seemed to focus on the symptoms rather than the real problem. There was no accountability at the highest levels. Decisions were made by consensus rather than independent actions. A glaring problem I honed in on was the isolation of upper management from mid-management. The director and his staff shrouded themselves in their little click while the branch chiefs ran the center.

The report is eight pages long, too long to publish here. However, here are a few excerpts from the report which illustrates the tone:

OFFICE OF THE DIRECTOR (Problem)

1. Two years ago our service center used far more overtime than any center in the nation. Our procedure at that time was to give each division an overtime allowance. When I compared our use to other centers it was obvious that we were squandering overtime.

   When the problem was brought to the attention of the director he moved the authority to approve overtime to his office. Our use of overtime dropped 50 percent. The problem of the division chiefs squandering their resources was not dealt with. They were not held accountable for their responsibility to mange their resources.

2. We (the center) were constantly late on getting our monthly budget projections to the Regional office on time. The various divisions consistently missed the 20th

of the month cutoff date for the submission of data to
my office. Also the Region continued to complain about
the poor data we were submitting.

When the problem became acute, the director moved the
division's cutoff date to the 15th of the month. This did
get the report to the Region on time. This also improved
the quality of the submissions because it gave my office
more time to review the data with the division and branch
chiefs. However, dealing with the problem by moving the
submission date was again a situation of dealing with
the symptom and not the problem. The problem was the
branch and division level managers were not held
accountable for meeting deadlines and reviewing their
own data to ensure its quality.

These are just a couple of the examples of the management problems I cited. At the end of each section I provided
recommendations for improving the efficiency of our
management system. At the end of the director's portion I
simply suggested a system to ensure completed staff action
was taken at each management level. Here is a sample of
what I suggested at the end of the directors section:

OFFICE OF THE DIRECTOR (Recommended solutions)
1. The director's office will not act on a problem which has
    been escalated to this level if completed staff action has
    not been done at each lower management level. As a
    minimum any problem forwarded to the directors office
    for action will include a statement of the problem, alter-
    natives considered, actions taken, the results of the actions
    and the reason the problem is being escalated to the
    directors level.

I knew my division chief, Bob Maddux like I knew the back of my hand. I knew he would never let my memorandum get to the director. Nor would he even broach any of the subject matter of the memorandum with the director. I gave him two weeks. I had not heard anything such as gnashing of teeth from the directors staff so I casually asked a couple of division chiefs what they thought of my suggestions in my memorandum. They said had not seen it. I had my secretary make seven copies of the memorandum and I hand carried a copy to each division office and the director's office. By the time I got back to my office there was a message from Bob, to come to his office immediately.

I went over to visit with bob. He was trying to be cool but his beet red face gave him away.

He asked," Why did you take it upon yourself to deliver that memorandum?"

I gave him the most wounded and puzzled look I could conjure up and said, "Bob. I found out that for some reason the director's staff had not seen my memo, so I just gave each of them a copy."

He sat there and looked at me for the longest time. The old saying holds true, "If looks could kill I would be dead." He finally said, "I wish you had waited for me to take care of that."

"Yea!" I thought to myself. "If I waited for you to distribute that memo I would have a long gray beard."

I asked, "is there anything else?" He gave me, "the look," again and replied with a curt, "No."

The director's staff didn't have much choice but to put my memo on their agenda. I am not naive enough to think that they would seriously consider anything I had said. I knew them well. I knew that they would thrash around in defense of themselves and during the process equate my mentality with that of a slug. I didn't care about their reaction. I felt I had performed one of the duties I was being paid to do, i.e., identify problems and make recommendations for improvements. I had my say. I said what I think they should have been told if they were serious about bringing about positive improvements. After the meeting of the director's staff my division chief couldn't wait to get to my office. He was in a totally different mood from the last time I saw him.

He had a big grin on his face when he said, "The director's staff discussed your recommendations and concluded there was no validity in them at all." I guess he expected a reaction. I think he wanted a reaction. I just looked at him. He went on to say, "If you had let me deal with your ideas in my way this could have been avoided." He turned and left my office. After he left I payed a visit to the only division chief at the time for whom I had any degree of respect. As soon as I walked into his office he started laughing.

He said, "Boy, did you stir up a hornet's nest. Your ears must be burning."

I said, "I take it from talking to Bob that you guys had a field day with my suggestions."

He said, "It was one of the more vocal meetings we've had." I offered to buy him a coffee and we took off to the cafeteria. There amid both of our laughing a lot he gave me a blow by blow description of the directors meeting.

Sometimes if you give things enough time things have a way of coming around. After I had retired an event occurred which vindicated a portion of my report. In my report I had pointed out the duplication of effort of the Program Analyst Staff in our center and the same staff in the Regional office. The district offices needed the Regional support because they did not have a staff of their own. I suggested the obvious which was get rid of the program analyst in the region assigned to support the center or eliminate the analyst staff in the Service Center. It happened. It didn't happen when I wrote the critique. It took years for the idea to finally sink in. They got rid of the regional analyst after I retired in 1988. Think of the amount of taxpayer dollars which could have been saved if the IRS had implemented this idea in 1979.

A Name by Any Other Name

The IRS has this thing about titles. I am a firm believer in KISS (Keep It simple Stupid) In the seventeen years I worked for the IRS I had my title changed four times. I was called a number of things, but officially I was called the Fiscal Officer, Management Analysis Officer, Financial Officer and back to Fiscal Officer. Periodically I received these changes to my title in the mail from the Personnel branch. Inasmuch as they didn't change my grade I didn't pay much attention to the changes. I just stuck them in my personal folder and waited for the next change. It did cross my mind to call Personnel and ask if they didn't have something better to do with their time. I never got around to it. If I had been wiser and more far sighted I would have requested them to change it one more time to what the job is now called. The comptroller. The name doesn't impress me but the two grade increase which went along with it, after I retired would have made a big impression on me.

There is only one way I can describe some of the office titles used within the IRS. They are sometimes pompous and sometimes just plan strange. In the National office there are a number of assistant to the Commissioner positions, a Deputy Commissioner and a bunch of associate commissioners. Somewhere there is a line drawn between what an assistant to the commissioner is and what an associate commissioner is. In the seventeen years I worked for the IRS I never could figure out what the difference was. I wonder if anyone really cares if a person is an assistant to or an associate. Behind all of this assistant to and associate jargon there are other titles tacked on like:

"Office of the Assistant Commissioner Human Resources Management and Support."

Can you imagine seeing this on letter heads? Why not apply KISS, (Keep It Simple Stupid). Call the position what it is, "Human Resources Division, National Office." This would cut the title in half.

Try this tongue twister. "Office of the Assistant to the Commissioner (Equal Employment Opportunity)."

KISS would simply make this, "Equal Employment Opportunity Office, National Office." Again the title has been cut in half and I think more clearly describes the office. I think there must be some kind of hidden agenda which dictates that all assistant and associate commissioners must have ten words in their titles. There is a kind of rhythm in the ten words in most of the titles. You can't say the IRS doesn't have rhythm!

Then there are the odd or interesting ones like, "Office of Disaster Recovery."

I would think this office would really be busy with the President and Congress declaring the IRS as a disaster. Is this the office one might call in the case of an atomic war, a terrorist attack, an earthquake or a bad hang nail. In the seventeen years I worked for the IRS I never did see this office go into action. Earthquakes happen all of the time in California. I didn't see them at any of the earthquake sites. Luckily I have never experienced an atomic bomb explosion. The IRS has suffered some terrorist attacks. The FBI was involved in these incidents. When does the, "Office of Disaster Recovery," go into action?

On a lighter note there is the, "IRP Branch." I think there are some acronyms that should be shied away from. There is the, Office of Acquisition." Do they really mean acquisition or do they really mean the, "Procurement Office? I could go on all day playing what is it with the IRS's titles. The last one I would like to share is, "The Office of Foreign Programs." Many people in the United States believe that most of the IRS's programs are foreign to them.

Gluttons for Punishment

Considering all that had transpired between the IRS and me over the seventeen years I worked for them, you would have thought that after I retired my name would have been stricken from all records and employees forbidden to speak my name. There must be a high degree of masochism in the organization. About one year after I retired I got a phone call from an employee development specialist (EDS) in the Training Branch. He wanted to know if I would consider teaching their retirement seminar. Our former Personnel Branch Chief had been teaching the class since his retirement a few years earlier. The EDS explained that they were looking for a new instructor because the former personnel chief might be a little too much in the old generation. He allegedly angered a few women in the classes by referring to them as gals and girls. Also the organization thought they were paying him to much and it was felt that he had a sort of monopoly on the class. I asked, "How much is he being paid." The EDS said, "Two hundred dollars per class." I told the EDS I would think about it and get back with him.

This presented me with two dilemmas. One was I had promised myself that I would never work again the rest of my life. I was just going to play tennis, racquetball, golf, fly and write. Even though I would only have to teach about two, one week classes each year the idea of the four letter word, "Work," didn't sit well with me. The second half of the dilemma was the organization was trying to get me to undercut and old close acquaintance of mine. I wasn't about to do that. I gave the thought of teaching the class some serious consideration. I think I let my ego make the decision. After all here they were coming to me asking, "would you like to teach this class for us? I decided I would do it. Not on their two hundred dollar terms, but on terms of what I thought my time was valued at. I considered what I would be paid at the current wage of a GS-12, step ten my old grade and step. I considered the prep and travel time. I had my figure . I called the EDS.

I started the conversation by saying, "It seems to me you have a bargain, if you are paying two hundred dollars to (the former personnel chief) to teach your class. Here is my offer," I went through the figures with him. When I had finished I said, "The bottom line is I will teach your class for six hundred dollars." I went on to say, "My time is to valuable to even consider a lesser figure." I was surprised. The EDS didn't hesitate or stutter. He said, "Its a deal. I'll send you the training package in the mail." That was in 1990. This is 2000. I know the Postal Service has this reputation of being slow. I am still waiting for the package to arrive. The truth is, when it had not arrived within a week I knew the deal was off. I can just imagine what happened when the EDS told the training branch chief about the commitment he had made to me. The response would have been, "Are you crazy? You fool. Do you know what you have done? There goes your annual award." Then the branch chief would have thought like a true IRS bureaucrat and said, "Hey. You didn't make that commitment in writing so we are off the hook. Act like nothing happened." They did and I did.

Why Seventeen Years

Why? Why would I work for the IRS for seventeen years when I thought so little of the organization and most of their managers? It could be I was trying to punish them for demeaning me by hiring me because I am black; It could be I liked playing win/lose games with small minded people; I may have liked the power of being an out of control employee in an organization with no controls; it could be because I was in a one of a kind job which gave me a lot of latitude. I could basically run my own show.

I wish I could subscribe to all or some of the above reasons for staying with the IRS. However, I think the truth is like many people I was caught in a personal situation whereas my family was comfortable and I was comfortable. I didn't have to commute three hours a day, as I did when I lived in The San Francisco Bay area. The cost of living in Fresno is probably a third less than the Bay area. Fresno is in reasonable proximity to the City (San Francisco) the coast, (Carmel) the mountains and the desert. The basic truth is it was easier to tolerate the IRS than to make major personal sacrifices by leaving Fresno. One more plus in my staying with the IRS was the time it gave me to gather the data to write, "A Token's View From Inside the Internal Revenue Service."

Reluctant Participants

It is expected for an author to give credit to those who have contributed greatly to the success of his book. However, there were no direct contributors to my book. There are a number of people in my book, "The good, the bad and the ugly," who made it possible for me to write this book. Inasmuch as all of the following managers are noted in my book, I want to offer them a special, thank you. Following are some, but not all of those who contributed;

Michael Dolan,
Deputy Commissioner of the IRS

We called him, "Big Mike," when he was an Assistant Regional commissioner in the Western Region. He was the person who agreed to and signed the agreement to give me a four–month developmental assignment for a higher position to get me to withdraw a complaint of discrimination. This turned out to be the best expense paid vacation my wife and I have ever had. (See chapter titled, "My Greatest coup.")

Thomas Cordoza,
Regional Commissioner Western Region

I want to thank Tom for understanding and acting on the problems which the Fresno Service Center EEO Ad Hoc committee presented to him. See chapter titled, "The Token Turns." I also want to thank him for not hiring me as his Regional

EEO Officer. I didn't want the job, but if I had been hired in the position I would have tried to develop a real EEO program for the Western Region. Because of the management climate of the IRS I would have failed and fallen into disgrace. (See chapter titled, "My Last Big Ha, Ha.")

WASSENAUR,
Assistant Regional commissioner, Administration

In my book I refer to WASSENAUR as, "Muck." It's much easier to write, and under the circumstances we met it seems quite appropriate. Muck took it upon himself to enlighten me on the popularity criterion inherent in the selection process of the Regional management Careers Program (RMCP). In as much as I wasn't very popular it was his enlightenment which convinced me I didn't want to be part of any careers program in the IRS. (See chapter titled, "Make me a star,")

Theron Polivka,
Director Fresno Service center

Theron thought EEO consideration was an inherent part of all management actions. I brought a different view to his attention by filing a complaint of discrimination. I must give him credit for adjusting his thinking and providing active consideration of EEO in lieu of inherent consideration. (See chapter titled, "Back to the Future,")

Fred Perdue,
Director Fresno Service center

I give Fred credit for reconsidering his position on the suggestions made by the EEO Ad Hoc committee. It may have taken almost a year and some persuasion from the Regional commissioner, but boy when he acted he acted. Some people have said he overreacted. (See chapter titled, "The Token Turns,")

Gary Mathews,
Assistant director Fresno service Center

I want to thank Gary for getting out of my business so I could do my job in resolving the horrendous payroll mess we encountered when the payroll center changed computer systems. (See chapter titled, "Payroll in the Renaissance.")

Joe Mc Clendon,
Budget Section chief Western Region

I want to thank Joe for his honesty and support in the few short years I knew him before he left the IRS.

Harvey Kuffner,
Chief Administration Division Fresno Service Center

Harvey was one of three division chiefs I worked for. Like myself, he didn't fit the IRS mold. He was honest and up-front. These are not traits which bode well for IRS managers. I thank him for being supportive of me in some trying situations. I was glade to see he was smart enough to leave the IRS and develop a new career.

Bob Maddux,
Chief Administration division Fresno service center

Bob was the second division chief I worked for. The best thing I can say about ob is he never had a clue. He reminded me of a man, perpetually walking around in the forest looking for the trees. I am indebted to Bob for many things, including being the catalyst which led to the IRS offering me a four-month expense paid vacation. (See chapter titled, "My Greatest Coup.") He also provided me with the opportunity to break the tedious boredom of every day work activities by filling some of my days with what I call, "Fun Things," in my book.

Glen Coles,
Chief Administration Division Fresno Service Center

Glen was the third and last division chief I worked for. Glen was a complicated person to work for. He was an IRS company man, but often he raised himself above the company mode and functioned in an honest and honorable way, i.e., like a normal human being. The two different sides of him appear in a number of chapters.

There are the many but nameless associates who contributed to this book. But because of the limited space and the fact I can't remember their names, they will remain nameless.